MW00364648

'Like the Rule of St Bened
carries far more wisdom than one might at first imagine. *The Way of Benedict* offers the reader an honest appraisal of how the author, who has been an enclosed Benedictine nun for more than a quarter of a century, has come to understand the monastic principles by which she lives. Even more usefully, she shares countless insights that can help those of us whose lives are un-cloistered to open ourselves to the many blessings that we so regularly miss. This is a book to read slowly, to read repeatedly, to share with friends and to give to any who long for more order, peace and joy in their daily lives.'
Stephen Cherry, Dean, King's College Cambridge

'This beautiful book introduces us to the Benedictine Rule as a wise way to live. Sr Laurentia outlines the teaching of St Benedict with great clarity and then suggests practical steps to live it out in daily life. In fractious times, this is a timely reminder that wisdom is universal.'
Abbot Christopher Jamison, author of *Finding Sanctuary* and *Finding Happiness*

'This book is a gift and a blessing for all of us, through Lent and indeed throughout the year. It is a treasure trove of beautiful and joyful moments alongside challenges and points for action that move us along our path. Reading it is like having a spiritual director sitting alongside you, encouraging and nudging you in a gentle way to turn again to face God. It is also profoundly practical and rooted in daily life, with examples that help us to reflect honestly on our relationships with God, with other people and with the earth. Like the Rule of St Benedict, there is "nothing harsh or burdensome" here. Instead, the book points us towards listening, gratitude and balance in our lives. It leads us towards a "radical way of living in, and engaging with, that world which God made and loves".'
Linda Jones, Head of Theology, CAFOD

'Readers ready for a fresh approach to Lent will appreciate finding eight blessings (though I found more) in *The Way of Benedict*. Sr Laurentia maps the route with gems from Scripture and the monastic tradition, inspiring us to "look forward to holy Easter with joy and spiritual longing", as Benedict's Rule teaches (RB 49:7). Taking Lent as both a liturgical preparation for Easter and a metaphor for our life's journey to God, she explores the blessings of bedrock practices such as worship and welcoming, as well as the subtler graces of new beginnings and going beyond our comfort zones. Always realistic about the hard work and personal growth needed to participate fully in the divine life, Sr Laurentia also reminds us of the loving God who is eager to bless even our smallest efforts. Readers who journey on *The Way of Benedict* might well discover not just a broader under-standing of Lent but also a livelier desire for resurrection.'
Mother Johanna Marie Melnyk OSB, Prioress, Holy Angels Convent, Jonesboro, Arkansas, USA

'The ancient wisdom of St Benedict has so much to offer today to anyone seeking to live more authentically in a world of constant change and turmoil. This book is born of deep engagement and attention to the profound desires of the heart and is a must-read for anyone seeking to understand the Benedictine way more deeply. Sr Laurentia writes beautifully, drawing the reader into a greater contemplation of the generous grace of God, whether starting out to understand, or an old hand at prayer. This is a Lent book that will be read for its joyfulness the whole year round.'
The Very Revd Dr Frances Ward, writer and theologian

Laurentia Johns is a Benedictine nun of Stanbrook Abbey, Yorkshire, England, where the main work is prayer and the praise of God. Since the 1990s, she has been involved in sharing the riches of the Christian monastic tradition with seekers of all kinds, including newcomers to the monastery, guests and oblates for whom she has also had pastoral responsibility. An experienced communicator on the Rule of St Benedict, Sr Laurentia has extended her ministry beyond the abbey via a variety of publications, talks, workshops, broadcasts and digital reflections.

THE WAY OF BENEDICT

Eight blessings for Lent

Laurentia Johns OSB

First published in Great Britain in 2019

Society for Promoting Christian Knowledge
36 Causton Street
London SW1P 4ST
www.spck.org.uk

For copyright acknowledgements, see pp. 122–3.

British Library Cataloguing-in-Publication Data
A catalogue record for this book is available from the British Library

ISBN 978–0–281–07581–2
eBook ISBN 978–0–281–07582–9

Typeset by Fakenham Prepress Solutions, Fakenham, Norfolk NR21 8NL
First printed in Great Britain by Ashford Colour Press
Subsequently digitally printed in Great Britain

eBook by Fakenham Prepress Solutions

Produced on paper from sustainable forests

In memoriam

Allen Johns
1932–2016

John A. Johns
1963–2017

Contents

Introduction

I am grateful to SPCK for the opportunity to reflect afresh on the Rule of St Benedict, one of the oldest guides in existence to living the Christian life. For Benedict (*c*.480–547), the life of a monk – we can say of any committed Christian – should always have a Lenten character (Rule of Benedict, henceforth RB, 49:1). We shall explore this idea below but it's worth stating at the outset that it definitely does not imply that Christian/ monastic life should be dour. Quite the opposite: orientated on eternity with God, all our days should be marked by 'joy and spiritual desire' (RB 49:7).

Two lines of thought converged to shape this book. First, the Lenten character of the Benedictine way suggested an approach that looks at the whole Rule.

Second, the invitation to write the book came at a time when I was preparing to celebrate my Silver Jubilee, a time of consciously counting blessings, one of the greatest of which for me has been living under the guidance of St Benedict. This prompted the idea of looking at the Rule as a series of blessings. But how to marry this with the Lenten theme? Providentially, a homily that I heard seemed to offer a synthesis, which made me think there could be some mileage in a Benedictine Lent book based on blessings.

Biblical scholars and theologians could fill tomes on the concept of 'blessing' but this particular preacher – himself no mean biblical scholar – put it succinctly: a blessing is a smile of God. To receive that smile is to be bathed in the merciful love of God; it is to receive the gift of peace and everything good; it is to be blessed. The book of Numbers records how the Lord, via Moses, taught Aaron how to bless the people. He was to say to them:

> The LORD bless you and keep you;
> the LORD make his face to shine upon you,
>   and be gracious to you;
> the LORD lift up his countenance upon you,
>   and give you peace.
> (Num. 6.24–26)

God's blessing – a smile – and a eureka moment for me. Just as Lent is essentially about turning back to God, so, in order to receive God's blessing/smile, we have to turn to face God.

Each chapter in this book explores one way we can turn back to God and the blessings that flow from such a turning, not only through the 40 days of Lent but every day on the life-long journey to God.

The book unfolds in eight chapters, which, more or less in sequence, span the Rule of St Benedict. However, in order – I hope – to avoid superficiality, certain topics, for example prayer, reverence, a healthy use of time, are treated in some depth.

Benedict has no specific chapter on the Bible in his Rule: the Word of God illumines every page. As we live not simply on bread but by every word that proceeds from the mouth of God (see Deut. 8.3; Matt. 4.4), it seemed important for a Lent book to have a chapter devoted to Scripture. So Chapter 4, 'The blessing of the Word', departs from the pattern of the rest of the book to focus on this key theme.

Introduction

In so short a book, no attempt has been made to be comprehensive, neither is this a commentary on the Rule, but rather a series of reflections that will, I hope, encourage you to engage with the text yourself. It will probably be helpful to have a copy of the Rule at hand to read alongside each chapter. Various translations are readily available and one version may be found on the Stanbrook Abbey website, <www.stanbrook abbey.org.uk>.

I wish to acknowledge an unrepayable debt of gratitude to all who, by their lives, preaching or writing, have formed me in the Christian monastic way. The list extends from St Ignatius of Antioch, born in the first century, to Sr Aquinata Böckmann OSB and Fr Michael Casey OCSO, born in the twentieth century; it includes, especially, the inspiration of my own sisters from the foundation of our monastery in 1623 to the present day. Particular thanks are due to Henry Wansbrough OSB (Ampleforth Abbey), Alban Hood OSB (Douai Abbey) and Beverley Hallam, oblate of Stanbrook, for their encouragement and insightful comments on the text, as well as to Rima Devereaux and the team at SPCK for helping to deliver this book with the kindly professionalism of midwives. Finally, the Rule does not exist to preach itself. All the practices promoted by Benedict that we shall look at in this book – prayer, worship, *lectio divina*, service of others – open the heart to receive the Holy Spirit, that light which shines within to give the knowledge of the glory of God in the face of Jesus Christ (see 2 Cor. 4.6), the Word of God who became flesh for us. More than ever, our troubled world needs the blessing of the light and peace that stream from the face of Christ – *the* smile of God. My prayer is that, during Lent and beyond, the Rule of St Benedict may help us all to receive more deeply, and reflect more brightly, that blessing: the light of Christ.

Laurentia Johns OSB
Stanbrook Abbey, Yorkshire
Pentecost 2018

1

The blessing of beginning

First of all, whenever you begin a good work, beseech him, most pressingly, to bring it to completion.
(RB Prologue 4)[1]

Beginnings are not always obvious to us as blessings, or at least there's an ambiguity about them. There's the incomparable feeling of freedom on the first day of a holiday; the mixture of thrill and panic when faced with a new job or an empty page, and, at the other end of the spectrum, the pain of facing life without a loved one. The first step in any undertaking is often the most difficult. Isn't Ash Wednesday the most difficult day of Lent? Why should all this be so? It could be simply a question of temperament, but maybe the unease with beginnings is a symptom of a certain dis-ease more widely experienced by a humanity that has lost the easy confidence characteristic of children. Perhaps we fear failure; probably many of us at some time have known that reluctance to face the demands of the day that can be a sign of depression. If you feel that any of the above applies to you, then help for Lent and life might be at hand in the unlikely form of a sixth-century set of instructions for monks.

First of all, to borrow some words from St Benedict, 'don't be daunted immediately' (RB Prologue, henceforth Prol., 48) either by the venerability of the Rule or by the inevitable strangeness, at times, of so ancient a text. What St Gregory the Great (540–604) said of the Bible can be applied also to the Rule of St Benedict, perhaps because almost half of its content is scriptural: 'it is both shallow and deep, where a lamb may paddle and an elephant swim'.[2]

It is 30 years since I first read the Rule and was immediately struck by its power, and particularly drawn by the Prologue. I knew nothing about monastic life and had barely heard of St Benedict. At a crossroads in life, just emerging from a sharp experience of loss and depression, I suppose I was open to a change in direction. So when a friend gave me a slim copy of the Rule of St Benedict without notes, it was the sheer force of the text that hit me, revived in me something started but stalled, a desire for the fullness of life. My first encounter with the Prologue of the Rule marked the beginning of a stirring of a vocation to the life of a Benedictine nun. At the time, this worked at a level below rational consciousness. Now, after living and studying the Rule for many years, I hope to articulate a little more clearly how the Prologue 'works', how this beginning can be a blessing, beckoning each of us to new life. Where does its power lie?

St Benedict: life, times and resonance with today

Most of the little we know about the life of St Benedict comes from Book 2 of the *Dialogues* of St Gregory the Great, written around 590. Traditionally, Benedict is thought to have been born around 480 in Umbria, now central Italy. After dropping out of university, he lived as a hermit for some years, then began to attract disciples whom he formed into small monastic communities at Subiaco in the countryside near

Rome. Later, around 529, he founded a monastery at Monte Cassino, between Rome and Naples. It was here that he wrote the Rule, probably in stages, until his death, around 547.

Among St Benedict's aims in writing the Prologue to his Rule must surely have been to invite and inspire beginners, to get them on board the monastic enterprise of seeking to orientate their whole lives towards God. Then it was essential to set out the ideals that animate the more prosaic details of daily life described in the rest of the Rule. For those who turned up at St Benedict's abbey in the 530s–560s from war-torn and plague-stricken Italy, there must have been much to attract in what the Prologue holds out: the chance 'to enlist with the Christ the true king', 'to take up bright weapons of obedience' (v. 3), 'to pursue peace' (v. 17), to enjoy good days and eternal life (vv. 15 and 17), to build a life on the solid rock of Christ amid the shifting sands (see v. 33). Our own times are scarcely less troubled and even more unstable, so we can probably identify with some of these. The Rule's aims, as set out in the Prologue, are timeless, appealing directly to the most profound desires of the human heart for peace, wholeness, harmony with self, neighbour, God and creation.

In an age besieged by detail, the succinct way St Benedict sets out his teaching is definitely a blessing. The Prologue is like a route-planner where we find sketched briefly the itinerary to God, which the rest of the Rule fleshes out; a journey for which the gospel is our guide (see Prol. 21) and the Holy Spirit our inner compass. It is an uphill climb that both demands and creates purity of heart[3] in those who follow; but a climb fuelled by love. On the Benedictine way, the outer journey with others is made in tandem with an inner one to the heart where God awaits our awakening to his presence. So, paradoxically, this journey becomes 'easier' en route, not because the terrain becomes more gentle but because contact with God in prayer and the Bible, and making room for the neighbour, all work to expand the heart.

A closer look at the Prologue: a spirituality of the heart

Most scholars now agree that Benedict took much of the text of the Prologue from an earlier source called the Rule of the Master (RM). Compared with the Master's preliminary section to his Rule, St Benedict's Prologue is about a third as long, but of more interest is the nature of the content he has selected. Benedict has chosen to include the section from the RM that is richest in quotations from the book of Psalms, and the psalms as questions. But perhaps Benedict's own additions are even more revealing: each one focuses on the human heart. Lent can be seen as a workout for the heart, and Benedictine spirituality, in the tradition of the desert monks, is very much a spirituality of the heart. This may help explain why a sixth-century monastic document seems to speak to people of our day: in 1,500 years the human heart has probably not changed very much.

The opening four verses and verses 46–49 of the Prologue are St Benedict's own words. They give a succinct programme for Lent, often described and experienced as something of a battle with dark forces within and without, but opening out towards light and peace as we draw nearer to God or rather allow him to draw nearer to us. A closer look at these verses also provides a glimpse of Benedict's personal approach, which is stamped on the rest of the Rule.

Listen, my son, to the precepts of the master and incline
the ear of your *heart*; freely receive and faithfully fulfil
the instructions of a loving father, that by the labour of
obedience you may return to him from whom you have
strayed by the sloth of disobedience. To you, then, are
my words addressed, whoever you are, that renouncing
your own will once and for all will take up the strong
and shining weapons of obedience to fight for the true
King, Christ.
(RB Prol. 1–3)

Therefore we must establish a school of the Lord's service;
in founding which we hope to set down nothing harsh or
burdensome. But if, for good reason, for the amendment
of evil habit or the preservation of charity, there be a little
strictness of discipline, do not be at once daunted and
run away from the way of salvation which is bound to
be narrow at the outset. But as we progress in this way of
life and in faith, we shall run on the path of God's commandments, *hearts* enlarged and with an unspeakable
sweetness of love.
(RB Prol. 45–49)

'Listen . . .' – can there be a more arresting start to any book?
We don't know how long St Benedict hesitated, if at all,
before writing the first word of his Rule, but we can safely
assume that, following his own advice at the head of this
chapter, he had prayed before taking up his stylus. 'Listen'
sums up the whole Benedictine way. If we can stop, still the
mind and really listen to the opening sentence of the Rule,
we discover a blessing: we are not alone. We are made in

the image of a God who is three persons in communion, and the deepest need of each of us is to be in relationship. In English we lose something of the personal tone of the original (Latin) words of St Benedict, who uses the singular 'you', but we can still pick up the intimacy of the invitation in the words 'my son'. Benedict has chosen to begin his Rule with words almost, but not exactly, from Scripture. There are echoes of the Jewish Shema, 'Listen, Israel' (Deut. 6.4–5), but the opening is even more reminiscent of phrases from the Wisdom books: 'Listen, my child, to your father's instruction' (Prov. 1.8, NJB), with a parallel from the Psalms, 'Listen, O daughter; pay heed and give ear' (Ps. 45/44.11);[4] 'Listen, my child, take my words to heart' (Prov. 4.10, NJB); 'My child, be attentive to my words; incline your ear to my sayings' (Prov. 4.20).

Rather than poring over a concordance to construct his first sentence, it seems more likely that Benedict wrote from a heart steeped in the Scriptures and kept supple by contact with the living Word. In the biblical tradition, the heart is the seat of the intellect, will, decision-making and convictions. It represents the deep core of the person, the person's identity, so to listen with the heart implies listening at depth and with one's whole being.

But what does it mean to 'listen with the *ear* of the heart', literally, 'to incline the ear of the heart'? On one level it is simply an amplification of the opening command to listen. The phrase sounds a little strange in English, but Benedict's Latin *inclina*, 'incline', allows us to follow a thread back to the original Hebrew, *nata*, where it carries the sense of 'bending, inclining, drawing close'. In the Psalms it is used of God's actions, as well as those of the psalmist. For example:

I love the LORD, because he has heard
my voice and my supplications.
Because he inclined his ear to me,
therefore I will call on him as long as I live.
(Ps. 116/114.1–2, NRSV)

So while one can listen with the heart to music or to a landscape, to listen with the ear of the heart implies an interpersonal listening and a degree of intimacy, like that of a child leaning towards its mother's breast, or as friends converse 'heart to heart'. We shall come back to listening, but here we can note that when we listen in this deep way we are drawn into a dialogue with the Word of God, as were the disciples on the road to Emmaus. You'll remember how in that story in Luke, the risen Christ, like a skilful psychoanalyst, helped the disciples enter more deeply into their hearts by gently questioning them – 'What things?' – evoking a response that allowed him to shine the light of the truth of the Bible more deeply into their hearts, until later they 'burned' (Luke 24.13–35).

The name 'Jesus' never appears in the Rule but, as the Word incarnate, his voice permeates each page, inviting, challenging, consoling and always transforming by his purifying power.

The body of the Prologue, then, as edited by Benedict, emerges as a dialogue between God and the human heart, structured around Psalms 34/33 and 15/14: 'Who is there that longs for life?' (Ps. 34/33.12; RB Prol. 15) and 'Who shall dwell in your tent or rest on your holy mountain?' (Ps. 15/14.1; RB Prol. 23). These same two psalms were used for instructing candidates for baptism in the early Church.

This cardio-psalmic bias of Benedict's – and the whole book of Psalms is one long dialogue between God and the human heart – comes out very clearly in the Prologue. The italicized words have been slipped into the Master's text by Benedict:

> Let us open our eyes to the deifying light and attune our ears to what the divine voice admonishes us daily, crying out: *If today you hear his voice, harden not your hearts* (Ps. 95/94.7–8) . . . You have ears to hear, hear what the Spirit says to the churches. *And what does he say?* Come, my sons, listen to me and I will teach you the fear of the Lord.
> (RB Prol. 9–12)

Benedict is often happy to follow the Rule of the Master quite closely, so the departures he makes from this text can be telling. What does it indicate, then, when Benedict inserts into the Master's text at verse 10 of the Prologue those words from Psalm 95/94, chanted by the monks each night at Vigils, 'if today you hear his voice, harden not your hearts'? If the monks needed this daily admonition against hardening of hearts or spiritual deafness, then there's a good chance they were prone to exactly that! This can be reassuring for us – we are not the first generation to find listening difficult.

In a way, the whole monastic project is about trying to come to terms with, and overcome, that particular human disability that is one of the heart rather than of the faculty of hearing. Instead of trying to give an explanation for this disability and suggest its cure, Benedict, in the Prologue, models for us, in an incarnate, Benedictine manner, the way to healing through dialogue with God in Scripture – especially the Psalms – which is the daily medicine of the monks. During Lent, particularly, all Christians try to enter more deeply into this dialogue.

It can be helpful to remember when we get to the body of the Rule, with its sometimes precise stipulations, that the whole text is underpinned by this spirituality of the heart spelt out in the Prologue, and is therefore concerned with inner dispositions: desire, motivation and self-honesty. When we let God work on us at this level, everything else will follow.

Echoes

If you listen deeply, with the ear of the heart, you will catch other echoes in the beginning of the Rule. One takes us back to the primeval beginning of the book of Genesis, to the falling away of our first parents, the failure of Adam and Eve to listen, to obey (the words are similar in many languages, for example in Latin's *obaudire*, 'to listen', and *oboedire*, 'to obey'). Early Christian writers linked this disobedience, or lack of listening, with a deformation of the original blessing of humanity's creation in the image and likeness of God. Beneath the text, 'the labour of obedience will bring you back to him from whom you strayed by the sloth of disobedience' (RB Prol. 2), we can pick up reverberations of the Fall, humanity's freely – if heedlessly – chosen alienation from God.

However we view the Fall, we cannot deny we live in a world radically out of kilter. Although Christ's redeeming work of salvation has been accomplished, it is not always easy to see the outworking of that victory even in our own lives as believers. But God comes to call us again, ever seeking to bring out and restore in us that faint image of divinity and to enlist us as collaborators in establishing the kingdom. From wherever we may have wandered through neglect, poor choices, stress, busyness, God never tires of calling us back. Lent articulates this call for us each year, but it is one that continues without ceasing throughout our time on earth.

You may also detect in this opening section of the Prologue echoes of the Prodigal Father welcoming back his wayward son (Luke 15.11–32). We can also see in that story a reflection of God's merciful desire for the restoration of lost humanity as he sent his own Son into the world. Our return, like that of the wayward son, will require that we 'come to our senses' (see Luke 15.17), undergoing that change of heart/mind which is true repentance or *metanoia*. The term in Hebrew, *teshuva*, carries a sense of returning home. This is not a once-and-for-all step but a continual conversion, a daily setting out.

Lent, either the liturgical season or a more personal Lent, which can visit us at any moment, is a good time to find space again to listen anew for that inner voice calling us back to intimacy, showing us the way of life (RB Prol. 18–20). Somehow, these 'conversion' moments can be times of great energy; once again orientated towards God, we are pulled back into his orbit as if by magnetism. Remember the Emmaus disciples, heavy-hearted and no doubt slow-footed as they walked away from Jerusalem, but then *running* back to the city after their encounter with the risen Christ. A similar force – notice how often the word 'run' appears – energizes the Prologue until, in Benedict's words, 'with hearts expanded, we shall run with the unutterable delight of love on the path of God's commandments' (RB Prol. 49).

Some blessings of beginnings

There is a particular blessing in beginnings, marked by great energy. Whatever the current state of the Big Bang theory, the biblical account of creation is ablaze with light and an explosion of life. Or think of the terrific dynamism of the early Church community forged from tongues of fire igniting thousands of conversions (Acts 2.41; 4.4). For each believer, too, there have been strong moments of grace, starting with the most powerful: baptism. Near the start of his ministry, Pope Francis charged those attending an audience in St Peter's Square with the task of finding out the date of their baptism. This can be a revivifying thing to do as we reflect on our incorporation into the life of Christ.

Then there are other beginnings, perhaps a conversion experience, a commitment in marriage or to a community, recovery after illness, a new start after some failure. To revisit and reflect on these times prayerfully is to re-access the original grace. Far from an exercise in nostalgia, to do this is to tap into the power of the eternal now of God's kingdom to which we already belong in Christ. One Christian husband and wife I know celebrate their wedding 'anniversary' every 100 days as a means of renewing their love.

We need endless new starts – perhaps this is partly what lies behind the Rule's dictum that the life of a monk should be a continual Lent, a continual new start (RB 49:1). St Benedict prescribed that the entire Rule be read aloud to aspirants three times during their periods of formation (RB 58), and he wanted the Rule read to the monks 'frequently' (RB 66:8). Today, in most monasteries a portion of the Rule is read aloud each day; many follow the four-monthly cycle of Rule readings, which is also used by Benedictine oblates who try to live the spirit of the Rule in the world. During a monastic lifetime the Prologue is heard numerous times. For me, it has never failed to inspire; each time offers a chance to begin afresh, another opportunity to respond to God's mercies which are new every morning (Lam. 3.22–23).

The Lord's path to glory was not one supersonic upward flight, but traversed a rocky way of setbacks, humiliations, suffering and death, and has blazed a trail for us to follow. As the saying goes, a monk is one who on rising each day says, 'Today, I begin', surely in the slipstream of Christ's resurrection. Gradually, through the work of the Holy Spirit, we may come to find we are less tense about beginnings than we used to be. Little by little, no matter what time does to the outer person's body, we can even begin to feel younger inside, more confident about new starts, with something of the fearlessness of the child. Perhaps this was one of the things Christ meant by saying that we need to become like little children to enter the kingdom. Not that we become heroes, but we relearn our dependence on God as the super-ego of our independence falls away; Eden is reversed.

Benedict describes the Rule as a 'Little Rule for beginners' (RB 73:8). In this he is not being condescending; as far as we know, he didn't write another rule for 'proficients' or for advanced-level monks. The tag seems partly a function of Benedict's humility, the realization that in the things of God, mortals can only ever be beginners. Then there's the element of simplicity implied in the phrase about entering the kingdom as children, open and receptive. He seems to want his monks to be ever setting out zealously but steadfastly.

The Prologue has been called the annunciation to the monk, something at once deeply personal yet universal, inviting us, as was Mary of Nazareth, to be drawn body, mind and spirit into God's saving plan for humankind. Looking back, I think this is how the opening of the Rule engaged me; something, or rather *someone*, was beckoning. It was both a whisper and a shout and, in a most courteous yet insistent way, demanded my attention. Opening with 'Listen', taking in the Psalms, Prophets and gospel and ending in the 'kingdom', shorthand for the rule of God's love that Jesus Christ came to inaugurate, the Prologue spans and abridges the whole Bible: in the beginning was the Word; therein lies its power.

As such, the Prologue is not a beginning that we leave behind as a train leaves the railway station but one that undergirds the whole journey, reminding us why we set out, and with the capacity to rekindle motivation – a set of principles, if you like. Some languages show this power of beginnings more clearly than English. In the Latin *principio*, 'beginning', can be seen 'principle'; in the Greek *arche*, from which is derived 'archetype', we see the same dynamic. So, as we 'leave' the Prologue, we take with us this beginning as a blessing to light up the rest of the Rule as it guides us through Lent and life.

For reflection and action

Lord, May your grace inspire all our actions and sustain them to the end that every prayer and work of ours may begin in you and by you be completed.
(Collect for first Thursday in Lent, Stanbrook translation)

1 (a) Alone, or in a group, read the whole Prologue of the Rule prayerfully. See <www.stanbrookabbey.org.uk/page-ruleofstbenedict.html>.
  (b) Read the Prologue of St John's Gospel.
  (c) Read Genesis 1 and 2, followed by Revelation 21 and 22.
  (d) Read Luke 15.

2 Reread the RB Prologue, listening for echoes with any of the above or other parts of Scripture.

3 You may wish to remember, in a spirit of thanksgiving, a new beginning in your life. Perhaps find out the date and place of your baptism and make a pilgrimage, real or virtual, to thank God for this beginning.

2

The blessing of gospel living

Let us set out with the Gospel as our guide.
(RB Prol. 21)

The Rule of Benedict is not an end in itself; it is a way of living the gospel, the good news that Christ is alive and active in our world. As Christians we celebrate this good news primarily at Easter, and so Lent can be seen as the time par excellence for preparing to deepen our commitment to gospel living.

In the Prologue, Benedict sets out the goal of the monastic journey – fullness of life in God's kingdom. He uses the first two chapters of the Rule to assemble the pilgrims for this journey: the monks (RB 1) and the abbot (RB 2); then, in the third chapter, 'Calling the Brethren to Council' outlines a working structure for them.

Chapter 4 of the Rule, to which we turn here, breathes the blessing of gospel living into this skeleton in order that the community might become a living icon of Christ. Here Benedict spells out, at some length, the practicalities of such gospel living. So the 'heart workout' underpinning the Prologue is not training us for some Olympic event but is to help us to love God and one another more fully; that is, to live the gospel.

The equivalent chapter in the Rule of the Master, Benedict's 'template', is headed, 'The Holy Art'. Benedict replaced this lofty title with one more in keeping with his practical, down-to-earth approach: 'The Tools of Good Works'. The use of 'tools' is one of the things that marks us out as human beings; with them we build a culture. For Benedict, the 'tools' in this chapter include a wide range of practices, from moral precepts to prayer and spiritual reading. Their purpose is to build a culture of the gospel: to restore what is lost, to renew relationships and re-create the peace of Eden. Every Christian is called to enter into, and witness to, this transforming power of Christ: 'By our baptism into [Christ's] death we were buried with him, so that as Christ was raised from the dead by the Father's glorious power, we too should begin living a new life' (Rom. 6.4, NJB).

From earliest times, followers of Christ have been marked out by this new way of life. One of the first designations for Christians was as people of 'the Way', a way that sought to incarnate Jesus' teaching on love of God and selfless love of neighbour given to his followers as a solemn command. The book of Acts presents a beautiful picture of gospel life where, empowered by the Holy Spirit, the disciples were enabled to live together in continuity with the life they had lived with Christ on earth, praising God, praying together and holding all things in common. Although it quite quickly went wrong (see Acts 5.1–11), that vision has never ceased to inspire Christians who wish to live their baptismal commitment wholeheartedly. It is a fundamental inspiration for the monastic life. Further, by incarnating the gospel, monks, nuns and all committed Christians also preach the gospel with their lives, as each community becomes 'a God-enlightened space in which to experience the hidden presence of the Risen Lord'[1] and where that experience shines out to others.

What is the gospel?

Those of us who have grown up with the gospel may have become a little dulled to its impact. It can be a useful exercise in Lent to think about what the good news means to us. For me it can be summed up in one word: *resurrection*. On Easter morning, Christians of the Eastern Orthodox Churches traditionally exchange the greeting, 'Christ is risen!' To which the response chimes back, 'Christ is risen indeed!' This is the original 'breaking news' that Mary Magdalene was charged to take to the incredulous disciples that first Easter morning; news they later found to be too good to be true even when the risen Christ was standing in their midst (Luke 24.41). The resurrection of Jesus is the positive charge that transforms every negative in life. We can get so used to the phrases and formulae of the resurrection that it often takes a long tramp through the valley of the shadow of death for us to realize anew that, as St Paul assured the Corinthians, 'Christ has been raised from the dead, the first fruits of those who have died' (1 Cor. 15.20).

The fact that Jesus rose from the dead validated all that he taught before his crucifixion. It empowered those who encountered him in his risen body to share the news orally in words that then became the seedcorn of the texts of the New Testament. The good news is Jesus himself, as John's Gospel shows by the 'I am' phrases put on Jesus' lips, including 'I am the way, and the truth, and the life' (John 14.6) and 'I am the resurrection and the life' (John 11.25). Luke makes the point by showing Jesus fulfilling the prophecy of Isaiah:

The spirit of the Lord is upon me,
for he has anointed me

to bring the good news to the afflicted . . .
to proclaim liberty to captives,
sight to the blind,
to let the oppressed go free,
to proclaim a year of the Lord's favour.
(Luke 4.18–19, my translation)

This is the good news of salvation, of being rescued from all that threatens to engulf us. But it is good news that invites our response and that, in a sense, lies dormant until we accept the message in faith. You will remember how, after proclaiming that text from Isaiah quoted above, Jesus returned the scroll, sat down and said, 'This text is being fulfilled today *even as you listen.*' The gospel does not work like magic. Although, in Julian of Norwich's phrase, 'all shall be well' and even now, at the deepest level, is well, she reminds us that Jesus did not promise us a life free from trouble and persecution; rather he assures us that he has overcome whatever 'the world' may inflict on us (see John 16.33).[2] Our part is to have faith in Jesus' words. Through the power of the gospel we can trust this promise of good news made to us by Jesus on the eve of his darkest hour. The Word summons us today and every day to reopen our hearts to the revitalizing power of the gospel.

Zooming in on RB 4

In this section we look at some of the features of RB 4, before focusing on the demanding challenge of the gospel to love our enemies.

There are two ways: one of life and one of death. And there is a great difference between these two ways. The way of life is this: first, you will love the God who created you; second, you will love your neighbour as yourself. And whatsoever you might wish not to happen to you, likewise do not do to another.[3]

Made up of a mixture of active moral precepts and spiritual maxims that mirror the pattern of the Rule as a whole, RB 4 may be viewed as a kind of abridgement of the complete text. Christocentric, God-focused and earthed in the realities of everyday life, it is also probably the least overtly 'monastic' chapter of the Rule and bears striking resemblance to *The Didache* (quoted above), an early – possibly first-century – Christian text, thought by some to be a kind of manual of initiation for newcomers to Christianity. 'The Tools for Good Works' should therefore have something to teach all Christians.

The main thing any Christian community, be it family, parish or monastery, has to do is to follow the gospel precepts of love of God and love of neighbour. So the 'first' with which the chapter opens is not simply the first in a list but also the most important, the primary, fundamental commandment, which is then spelt out over the next 72 precepts. This is a typically Benedictine pattern: a strong, spiritual principle is stated, and then its practical applications developed. Imbibing the Rule over many years, we come to internalize this way of thinking so that when threatened by drowning in a sea of detail before a meeting, or a plethora of bewildering choices in life, we are able to identify the key principle and try to act accordingly.

Even so, a cursory reading of this chapter can leave us with an impression of a list of 'dos and don'ts', which may not be immediately attractive. We need to remember the context of the opening biblical text. The injunction to love God with all one's heart, soul and strength (Deut. 6.5), which forms the core of the Shema, the daily prayer of our Jewish brothers and sisters to this day, is a summary of the law, the Ten Commandments given to the Israelites via Moses and incorporated into Jesus' new law of love in the gospel (for example, Mark 12.28–34). Both laws are about freedom. Remember that the law was given to the Israelites *after* they had been miraculously rescued from slavery in Egypt, and commemorated by them subsequently each year on the Jewish feast of Pentecost. For Christians, the crossing of the Red Sea by the Israelites in the Old Testament came to represent baptism, the liberation from sin.

When Christians came to name the feast on which they celebrated the descent of the Holy Spirit on the first apostles, they did not have to cast about to find one: the existing Jewish feast of Pentecost already held that same resonance of freedom that the Holy Spirit brought. St Paul never ceases to link this gift of the Holy Spirit with our liberation from oppression by Christ's victory over sin and death: 'where the Spirit of the Lord is, there is freedom' (2 Cor. 3.17). Into this freedom we are baptized, so that for Christians the demands of love are not long lists to be obeyed but rather aids that stir up and motivate our actions from within. We are back to the dispositions and desires of the heart, of an inner drive rather than external coercion.

Remember that Benedict wished his monks to maintain a Lenten focus throughout their lives. This has many implications, but a key one is surely about growth in liberty of spirit as we mature in Christian discipleship.

At times in the life of each individual and every community or family, situations arise that demand sacrifices. We may have to relinquish cherished plans, or bear injustice or the fallout from difficult scenarios; we shall all certainly have to part with loved ones sooner or later. Usually, given grace and support, we will rise to these challenges. Perhaps even more demanding is the daily selflessness required for the long-term care of the chronically ill or elderly, or simply the challenge of being faithful in the face of our own diminishment of health or resources.

The night before his death, Jesus gave us an extraordinarily powerful example of what love of neighbour means in practice. His stooping to wash the feet of his friends elevates every least service we do for one another to the level of his self-giving love and becomes a blessing for us. The account of this scene in John's Gospel holds another beatitude: 'If I, your Lord and Teacher, have washed your feet, you also ought to wash one another's feet. For I have set you an example . . . If you know these things, you are blessed if you do them' (John 13.14–15, 17).

Verses 10–19 of RB 4 sketch out some of the concrete ways we can serve our neighbour in what are traditionally called the corporal works of mercy: relieving the lot of the poor, clothing the naked, visiting the sick, consoling the sorrowful and so on.

Gregory Collins OSB has brought out the intimate link between such self-emptying love (*kenosis*) and the creation of Christian community/communion (*koinonia*).[4] Put simply, it is the love of Christ which gathers us together, not into a 'club', be it never so holy a one, but into a spiritual communion, and the nature of that Trinitarian love is to pour itself out selflessly for others.

There is no question of our being able to fulfil these obliga-tions of love by sheer willpower through gritted teeth; it is only Christ working in us through the gift of the Holy Spirit who can empower us to act. 'To prefer nothing to the love of Christ' (RB 4:21) is a guiding precept of this chapter and the whole Benedictine ethos. The way the spiritual precepts such as listening to holy readings (v. 55) and turning often to prayer (v. 56) are interspersed among the more practical demands in this chapter highlights our need to nourish within us the life of Christ, our baptismal grace, so that we grow in love.

This love needs to be purified, strengthened, trained to become ever more free. Each year, the 40 days of Lent provide an education in freedom, so that gradually our loving service of God and neighbour may, we hope, well up from deep within as if spontaneously but in reality under the irrepressible power of the Holy Spirit.

Living in the landscape of the Beatitudes

In RB 4 we are in the landscape of the Sermon on the Mount, with its compelling and exacting demands that make up the terrain of our Christian practice. Just as Jesus, at the start of his ministry, charted the constitution of his new kingdom centred on the radical reversals of the Beatitudes, where the poor and indigent are called 'blessed', so, near the start of the Rule, it seems that St Benedict wishes the criteria for gospel living to be proclaimed clearly. For this chapter probably more than any other, the Rule draws on the voice of the Word: almost every phrase in RB 4 is a quotation from or an allusion to Scripture. So here we find ourselves automatically making use of the chapter's fifty-fifth tool: 'listen readily to sacred readings'. In the original Latin, the text of this chapter is set out more like poetry than prose. Rhyme, rhythm and alliteration make for easier memorization and facilitate the inscribing of the law of love on the human heart.

And this is the heart of the matter: the command to love our enemies. Do we admit that we have enemies, or quite often one enemy at a time? Beyond irritations, minor or massive, and irrational antipathies, there may well be people who actually will us harm and wish we didn't exist. And, if we are honest, we may perhaps harbour similar thoughts about others, or at least one other.

Lent provides an opportunity to face up to difficult relationships. An internationally renowned retreat-giver once related how someone he was accompanying came to realize that the one who induced in her feelings of oppression and unease was her husband. These sorts of levels of domestic antagonism are not unknown in monasteries or in any human institution. We should not despair: it is precisely from such prisons of darkness and concealment that Jesus has come to liberate us. Where there is honest recognition of a problem and the desire for reconciliation, combined with faith in Jesus' power to act through the Holy Spirit, the counsel of a wise guide and much patience, miracles can happen. As Benedict had already made clear in the Prologue, 'what is impossible for us by nature, let us ask the Lord to supply by the help of his grace' (Prol. 41).

This chapter supplies some of the key tools necessary for the process of learning to love one's enemies, one of which is pre-emptive and even preventative: to make peace before sunset (RB 4:73, see Eph. 4.26). While we are usually quick to gloss over offences caused by our friends, the regular oiling of less cordial relationships with an unfussy, sincere apology can prevent the rusting of charity.

Another simple tool – which is not to say an easy one to apply – is to speak well of one's enemy. In Latin, *benedicere* literally means 'to speak well of', and the same word means 'to bless' (RB 4:32). As followers of Christ, we cannot wait for the world to be nice to us before we afford each person the justice they deserve from us as fellow children of God. If, acting out of prayer and strengthened by grace, we can remain silent, even if seething within, and thus 'simply' desist from the natural reaction of retaliation to slights and insults visited on us, then that is a step in the right direction. If we can stick to Benedict's counsel about using the tools 'unceasingly', we may even find ourselves congratulating our 'enemy' on some achievement or commiserating with them in some misfortune. Then, as grace builds on grace, and with continued prayer and practice, we can in time find springing up a genuine affection for someone we could once barely tolerate in the same room (see 1 Pet. 1.22).

In a world where we can often feel powerless to effect change, each of us has the capacity to augment or deplete the world's resources of peace (see Jas. 3.5–6) simply by how we speak of and with others. It is striking that no fewer than nine of the tools in RB 4 are concerned directly with the quality of a monk's speech (vv. 7, 28, 32, 39, 40, 51, 52, 53, 68).

Repeated failure should not weaken our desire for growth in this area of difficult relationships. Our growth in the Spirit, or rather the deepening of the Holy Spirit given to us in baptism, tends not to follow a direct upward trajectory but rather circles round. The text of RB 4 seems to reflect this as the precepts around love of the neighbour, including the enemy, which we might expect to find grouped together in one section, are interspersed through the chapter:

'Do not do to another what you do not wish done to yourself' (v. 9).

'Do not relinquish charity' (v. 26).

'Love your enemies' (v. 31).

'Live by God's commandments every day' (v. 63).

'Pray for your enemies out of love for Christ' (v. 72).

'If you have a dispute . . . make peace before sunset' (v. 73).

From our perspective of living in the maelstrom of human relationships, this circling pattern can appear as a going around in circles, or even a bashing of heads against brick walls. But when we look more closely, and often only with hindsight, it is possible to discern a development in our lives that this chapter maps out: we move from the truce-like position of mutual self-preservation, 'do not do to another what you do not want done to yourself' (v. 9), to becoming positive peace-makers who share in God's life, 'Blessed are the peace-makers, for they will be called children of God' (Matt. 5.9). Motivated by the love of Christ, we become caught up into the gentle tornado of the Holy Spirit, God's love in us (Rom. 5.1–5).

Blessings of gospel living

To hear and respond to the call to follow Christ is a deeply personal experience, but it is always a call to live out the gospel with others. Our baptism binds us into the body of Christ in so profound a way that the most remote hermit on the most isolated island is not outside this incorporation. One of the more urgent challenges of our day, for society as a whole and Christians in particular, is how to reach out to those who feel they do not belong and who have a sort of 'hermithood' thrust upon them.

Loneliness is a scourge for a social species, and Benedict would surely endorse a new precept: 'to include the lonely'.

Meanwhile, for those of us who live in the hurly-burly of community/family life there are other challenges. St Augustine, a major source behind the Rule, wrote of Psalm 133/132 that it 'made the monasteries'. It would take a whole book to explore that sentence, but we can sense what he may have meant by reading the psalm:

> How good and how pleasant it is,
> when brothers live in unity!
> It is like precious oil upon the head
> running down upon the beard . . .
> Like the dew of Hermon, which runs down
> on the mountains of Sion.
> For there the LORD bestows his blessing:
> life forever.

This psalm allows us to see in metaphor the goal of gospel living: eternal life, the unsurpassable blessing at the heart of every blessing, that of sharing in the life of the Trinity. We glimpse this at the best moments of our communal life, be it in the family, parish or in our friendships, even now. Who hasn't experienced at some time one of those golden days where time seems to both stand still and slip by speedily; where there is shared laughter, genuine kindness and silence full of communion? But the psalm also implies the way to this blessing; that is, by 'dwelling', 'remaining', 'abiding' in our relationships, even, and especially, when they are difficult or seemingly impossible. St Paul knew that our very powerlessness can be a source of strength as we have to call on the Lord for help: 'for whenever I am weak, then I am strong' (2 Cor. 12.10). I am surely not the only one who tends to make this cry for help a last resort! But God is patient and we are 'never to despair of his mercy', as runs Benedict's final tool for good works (RB 4:74).

In so far as our difficulties in loving our neighbour throw us more into the arms of Christ, our very failures in gospel living can become a blessing. But we do have to use these tools of gospel living every day, as Benedict reminds us in RB 4:76, for the fourth time in this chapter.[5]

To concentrate on the daily is very much part of the Benedictine way, where the word 'every day' (*cotidie*) appears eight times across the Rule as a whole. If you have accompanied a loved one through terminal illness, you will know the wisdom of this 'daily' emphasis, which helps us to live as fully as possible a day at a time. Often, one sees brave souls discovering, perhaps for the first time since childhood, the joy of living each day as a gift. For Christians there is also the strengthening vista of eternal life after death, while something of this new life can break through even into current, difficult circumstances.

St Paul was acutely aware of this continuum of present-day circumstances with eternal life, as his second Letter to the Corinthians shows. Flowing from Christ's sacrificial death, the grace to live with the new life of Christ's resurrection is a profound blessing of gospel living, a blessing that motivates us to live as Christ lived. Christ's purpose in dying for all, wrote St Paul to his friends in Corinth, was 'that those who live might live no longer for themselves, but for him who died and was raised for them' (2 Cor. 5.15).

Once we have reached this conclusion, 'the love of Christ becomes the motive force in our lives' (2 Cor. 5.14), and 'though our outer humanity is in decay yet, day by day, we are inwardly renewed. Our troubles, slight and short-lived, are preparing us for an eternal weight of glory which far surpasses them' (2 Cor. 4.16–17, my translations).

So our daily steps in trying to love God and neighbour, in accordance with gospel precepts, are leading us to something ineffable, to something, in the words with which Benedict chose to conclude RB 4, 'no eye has seen, nor ear heard – what God has prepared for those who love him' (see 1 Cor. 2.9).

For reflection and action

O God, whose wonderful grace enriches us with every blessing, grant that by passing from our old ways to newness of life, we may be prepared for the glory of your heavenly kingdom.
(Collect for fifth Monday in Lent,
Stanbrook translation)

1 In a group, read the Gospel of St Mark aloud, straight through around the group. It takes about 100 minutes. After some silence, you may wish to share your responses to the reading.
2 Choose six tools from RB 4 for your personal spiritual tool-kit. Pray and work on one for each week in Lent.

3 **Re-new**
Created, each one of us, beautiful
    and blessed,
in the image and likeness of the
    One who created us,
God is our refuge, and still takes
    sanctuary in us.

Graced by humility to retrieve the
    lost kindness in our own eyes
can we see ourselves and others as
    God sees us.

In solidarity we walk with those on
    the road, whose burden is heavy
and whose loss is great.

Can we bless the imagining
    of ourselves
which is so often smaller than God's
so that each of us might see
    that future
and that stature that we are called
    to become.

Make us attentive still to good news
and small occasions.
To the grace of what is possible.
That we may neither miss our
    neighbour's gift
nor our enemy's need.

(From *Crossing Barriers*, Week of Prayer for
Christian Unity, 2017)[6]

3

The blessing of attentiveness: RB 5–7

We shall not be heard for our many words but for purity
of heart.
(RB 20:3)

Attention Deficit Disorder (ADD) is a condition that can
affect especially children, but most of us will be familiar with
variations on the story of someone who sets out to do a job,
say, strimming the lawn, and is deflected by a thousand other
demands so that by the end of the morning they are exhausted,
surrounded by a series of half-completed tasks while the grass
remains unstrimmed. It is often the same in our spiritual lives.
The spiritual attention deficit we experience, while no doubt
abetted by the pace of modern life, is not confined to our age
but is, rather, a malady of the human heart in its fallen, divided
state. The monastic foundress Dame Gertrude More wrote in
the seventeenth century:

From multiplicitie and dejection
that would breed our soules confusion,
defende us Lorde with thy Benediction.[1]

A powerful antidote to this divided heart is attentiveness or
mindfulness, which can be seen as the thread linking chapters

5 to 7 in the Rule of St Benedict on 'obedience', 'silence' and 'humility'.

It could be easy to skip over these three chapters as being more for monks and nuns, but that would be a mistake, for here we touch the essence of Benedictine spirituality, which has a far wider hinterland than the monastery grounds. As we saw in Chapter 1 of this book, 'obedience' is about a deep attentiveness, a listening 'with the ear of the heart' that takes us below surface appearances. The sort of attentiveness fostered in the Rule is about trying to catch the loving melody of God's providence in the events of life. For the novice, this may be the challenge of carrying out an uncongenial obedience, trusting that God's will is being carried out through the superior's command. But whatever our vocation, we shall be faced with situations that will demand of us a deep faith-filled listening to the God who loves us. It can take a long time to reach the place of acceptance. What we are always listening for is the truth that sets us free (see John 8.32). This process of deeply attentive listening is facilitated by 'silence', both outer, material silence and the degree of silence in our hearts. Silence 'earths' us in truth, which is what humility is all about. And the deepest truth, as a wise contemporary abbot has said, is that we are humble dust created by our loving God and destined, through his mercy, for glory. St Benedict says as much in the Prologue (Prol. 6–7).

There are excellent commentaries and books on each of these three chapters,[2] but here I would like to suggest that they can be taken together as a triad that mirrors the dynamic of prayer shown by Jesus himself.

Not everyone is called to vowed obedience but all are called into a deeper relationship with God. We sense this by the failure of anything less than God to satisfy our deepest aspirations. So inasmuch as RB 5–7 offer a mini treatise on prayer, these chapters can help us on the inner journey to unity.

In order to get to grips with the concept of 'purity of heart', central to prayer, we shall need to explore the desert tradition, one of the main sources from which the Rule springs.

But first a word on 'attentiveness' or 'mindfulness' – the terms are virtually interchangeable – which may be defined at its simplest as 'the quality or state of being aware of something'; we could add, 'in order to act consciously' rather than in sleepwalker mode. As is well known, there has been a great flowering of interest in mindfulness over recent years, perhaps not unconnected to the speed of life and the heedlessness that haste can spawn. Mindfulness seems to be a practice that appeals to people across a wide spectrum of religious and non-religious backgrounds and has even been recognized by health authorities as a possible therapy for depression. Benedictines can feel at home with such a concept, elements of which, such as 'remembering' and being attentive to one's inner drives and motivations, form part of our Judaeo-Christian heritage. A significant difference for the Christian is that it is never a question of practising mindfulness for its own sake or in abstract, but is rather always about our being mindful of God and his works, including ourselves. For that reason, the term 'attentiveness' or 'attention' is perhaps more helpful for our purpose. Derived from the Latin, *attendere*, its original meaning was 'to stretch out something', for example a hand, '*towards* something or someone', so the word implies an object or a relationship. This idea is perhaps not as strongly present in the word 'mindfulness'. For Simone Weil (1909–43), every act of attention (presumably towards a good object) aids prayer.[3]

The desert tradition

In the early centuries, Christians went out to desert places in droves to seek God, sensing that they needed to withdraw from their busy lives and that a certain solitude and freedom from distraction would aid their search.[4] They found instead their distracted selves! They found that they became angry over little things – the smashed water jug, the broken stylus – even when there was no one around to blame. And, fortunately for us, they were humble enough to admit these failings and to share their acquired wisdom with others wishing to seek God. The practice of 'manifestation of thoughts' developed, where inexperienced monks would share with a trusted elder their inner thoughts and temptations. Thus, a whole science of attentiveness to the movements of the human heart was worked out, passed on and recorded in various *Lives* and collections of the sayings of the Desert Fathers.[5]

We learn from St Athanasius that 'attention' was a key theme in the teaching of the great pioneer monk St Anthony of Egypt in the third century, whose last exhortation to his monks was said to be 'attend/pay heed to yourselves'.[6] Evagrius of Pontus (345–99) was one of the first monks to articulate this teaching in writing. He describes, with great insight, the eight main inner drives or 'thoughts' of the human heart: gluttony, lust, anger, covetousness, pride and so on, and how they block spiritual growth.[7] His disciple, John Cassian (*c*.360–435), another major voice behind the Rule of St Benedict, systematized much of this teaching, which he had experienced during the years he spent at the feet of various elders in Egypt and Palestine in his younger days. Cassian did not originate the teaching on the thoughts or passions but he did make some significant changes in the vocabulary used in this field, which are worth exploring.

Evagrius had used the term *apatheia*, or 'passionlessness', for the state of freedom from domination by passions/thoughts, which was the aim of the desert monks and nuns. Cassian, perhaps realizing that passionlessness is not the easiest of concepts to grasp, turned things round. What is it to be free from these assaults of the human passions that throw us off our desired goal of focusing on God? It is, he sensed, to be 'pure of heart'; 'pure' in the sense of 'unalloyed', and so to be undivided, unified within. This is far from the Stoic overtones of passionlessness and is rooted in Scripture.

> Create a pure heart for me, O God;
> renew a steadfast spirit within me.
> (Ps. 51/50.12)

The term 'purity of heart' retains that spirit of fervour and desire so essential to the spiritual life and that passionlessness, misunderstood, might extinguish. We do not need to put out all passion; indeed, to do so would be injurious, since desire is an essential component in our journey to God, as St Augustine taught.[8] Instead, we need rather to let these passions be puri-fied and unified. 'Blessed are the pure in heart, for they will see God' (Matt. 5.8).

What the early Christian/monastic tradition shows is that our desire to grow closer to God must be matched by a growth in self-knowledge. The Desert Fathers sometimes spoke of prayer as the monk's 'mirror'.

Prayer in the Rule of St Benedict

It is often noted that there is little in the Rule of St Benedict about personal prayer. Chapter 20, 'On Reverence in Prayer', fills barely ten lines. But the whole way of Benedict, as outlined in the Prologue, can be taken as a return journey to God not only in the next life but as a growing union with God now through prayer.

The Rule offers glimpses of monks slipping into church alone outside the times for communal services, or staying in church after a service to pray personally (see RB 52:3–4). Prayer crops up, or is implied, in other places in the Rule, for example as one of the 'tools of good works' (RB 4:56) and, in a particularly strong, even if not a specific way, in the chapters we are looking at here (RB 5–7). Then there is Benedict's suggestion that an increase in personal prayers may be something the monk might offer during Lent (RB 49:5). There is something refreshing about the freedom that seems to be afforded Benedict's monks when it comes to personal prayer. This freedom is not at odds with the deep reverence Benedict advocates when we approach God in prayer.

The 'fear of the Lord', which marks the first three rungs of the ladder of humility in RB 7, is not a cringing or servile fear. Rather, it suggests a sense of awe, which Julian of Norwich calls 'reverent dread' and is characteristic of any deep love where respect for the mystery of the person and a fear of causing hurt or offence combine.

The spiritual heart of the Rule: RB 5–7

The image of a ladder, traditional symbol for our connection with God since at least the book of Genesis (Gen. 28.12), links these three interrelated chapters. RB 5, on obedience, opens: 'The first rung of the ladder of humility is obedience without delay. This comes naturally to those who hold nothing dearer than Christ' (RB 5:1–2). At the end of RB 7, on humility, we are given a portrait of a monk on the top (twelfth) rung of the ladder, based on that of the publican in the Temple at prayer, someone aware of his sinfulness and who goes home at rights with God through his honest self-assessment or humility (see Matt. 8.8; Luke 18.13). In between comes RB 6, on silence, or more accurately, 'restraint of speech', which allows the monk to practise attentiveness to God in prayer, to Scripture, to the abbot and brethren and to the innermost workings of his own heart.

So these three chapters scale the entire trajectory of a monk's spiritual life, from entering into the silence of the monastery, persevering over many years in obedience, which gradually loosens the power of his negative drives until, 'having ascended all the steps of humility, the monk will soon arrive at that perfect love of God which casts out fear' (RB 7:67). Someone who, as we read in the closing verse of chapter 7, has been purified by the Holy Spirit, is growing in that purity of heart that allows us to perceive something of God. Such a person realizes with St Paul that prayer is not something we do but rather something the Holy Spirit does in us (Rom. 8.26–27). The last verse of RB 7 indicates how this transformation has come about: 'All this will the Lord by the Holy Spirit deign to manifest in his labourer now purified from vices and sins' (RB 7:70). As you will detect, this language echoes the desert tradition.

The eight principal thoughts/vices are not spelt out in the Rule, though it seems the monks would have heard passages of Cassian's writings read aloud after supper (RB 42:3), but chapters 5–7 of the Rule certainly put us in touch with that tradition. (See RB 6:3; 7:10–13, 29, 44, 67–69.) In case we suspect that all this looking at oneself is narcissistic, it's worth looking at the prayer printed at the end of this chapter. Taken from Cassian's tenth Conference, 'On Prayer', it shows the goal of all the work on the inner self: that God should be all in all.

How can Benedictine spirituality help us to pray today?

I would like to suggest three ways:

1 by giving a clear focus to our spiritual life;
2 by providing the sort of environment where prayer can take root;
3 by enabling us, especially through the lens of attentiveness in RB 5–7, to detect something of the inner dynamic of prayer.

1 A clear focus

Whoever you are, hastening to your heavenly homeland . . .
(RB 73:8)

It's helpful to think of RB 5–7 on the inner life of the spirit as part of the bigger picture of the whole Rule. We get distracted when we forget our priorities, the goal of the journey or that we are on a journey at all.

While to live in the present moment is generally a helpful spiritual maxim, it can be easy to get bogged down in the present with its many, often conflicting, demands and some-times seemingly intractable difficulties. This is where the Rule, and especially the Prologue, can be useful in reminding us why we set out – we are seeking fullness of life, eternal life, by returning to God. So the Rule reminds us of our goal and reconfigures our journey.

Attentiveness to the 'now' needs always to be balanced by the pull of the 'beyond'.

Then, to be focused, we need a focus. We can delude ourselves that if only we had more time, space, silence or whatever, we'd finally get our spiritual lives in order, but anyone who has seen a mother with a baby or small child knows that it is possible to be both busy and focused when you have a clear focus. The bond of love between mother and child somehow frees up the mother to multi-task.

The Rule's strongly christocentric thrust is always drawing us back to Christ than whom nothing is to be preferred (RB 4:21; 5:1; 72:11). Once more, this is gospel teaching: 'Whoever loves father or mother more than me is not worthy of me,' says Jesus (Matt. 10.37). This is not at all to denigrate the bonds of family love (remember Jesus took to task the Pharisee who tried to avoid responsibility towards his parents; see Matt. 15.3–9) but underlines the radical call of being a Christian.

2 The right environment

If it is only when a monk stands in prayer that he prays, such a one does not pray at all.
(Saying of a Desert Father[9])

The early monks and nuns aimed at continual prayer and in this they were following the teaching of St Paul, who had urged the Thessalonians to pray continually (1 Thess. 5.17). As Christians, we aspire to grow through grace into that intimacy with the Father that belongs to Jesus as Son. Such continual prayer does not mean being on our knees 24/7, but rather involves becoming increasingly aware of, attentive to, the gift of prayer that is already ours in the Spirit through baptism.

The Rule provides many aids to this process: a quiet environment, regular calls to liturgical prayer, an immersion in Scripture and an ethos of trying to do all things attentively.

For the Benedictine monk and former spiritual father of my own monastery, Dom Augustine Baker (1575–1641), every practice in the Rule, every going to choir, every obedience, *lectio divina*, fasting, silence, vigils, the practice of personal prayer, were all means to the end of union with God. Perhaps we could say 'means to the end of "Prayer"' with a capital 'P'.[10]

Without doubt, it is more of a challenge to find a climate so favourable for prayer in our often frenetic world. So it is impressive to see how creative those who decide to adopt the spirit of the Rule can be in fostering a Benedictine micro-climate to help their spiritual lives, for example by punctuating the working day with parts of the Divine Office or making regular retreats. To find strongholds of silence in what can seem the norm of noise in Western culture certainly demands determination and ingenuity. One oblate I know, a health professional, has taken to arriving a few minutes early for home visits so as to build into her day some sanctuaries of silence. Another prays the office during his commute to London. A third gets up early to fit in a prayer walk before work.

Mindful that RB 6 is about 'restraint of speech' rather than absolute silence, it is good to recall that there are some forms of noise over which we have more control. We can decide when and how to speak, when to turn off the phone, tablet or computer. Lent is a helpful time to review our use of these modes of communication and to ask ourselves whether we might carve out for ourselves more space and freedom by limiting their use.

3 'Pure prayer'

Three times in RB 20, Benedict uses the word 'pure' in relation to prayer: we are to pray 'with all humility and pure devotion' (v. 2), and prayer is to be 'short and pure' (v. 4). Between these two, like a hinge, Benedict sets 'purity of heart'. This is the quality that the early monks prized so highly and that John Cassian made the first goal of all the monk's grace-supported endeavours. His aim was not to make purity of heart an end in itself but something essential for the ultimate goal of what he called 'the Kingdom of Heaven', meaning union with God or the beatific vision – heaven itself. 'Purity' here does not mean a physical property or sexual purity, but rather pure in the sense of unmixed, unalloyed. So perhaps 'singleness of heart', through which we grow in inner unity, is a helpful way to think of the concept.

The prophet Malachi has a powerful image of the silver refiner sitting at his task of skimming off all the impurities from silver: the Lord, at his appearing, 'will sit as a refiner and purifier of silver, and he will purify the descendants of Levi and refine them like gold and silver, until they present offerings to the LORD in righteousness' (Mal. 3.3). Apparently, once the refiner is able to see his face reflected in the molten silver, the metal is 'pure'. Not only shall the pure in heart be blessed as they shall see God, but God shall see restored in them the image of his Son. 'When he is revealed, we will be like him, for we will see him as he is' (1 John 3.2). 'Purity of heart' evokes all the mysterious inner workings of prayer on the inner self as we become more unified within.

In the second century, St Irenaeus of Lyons (c.130–200) famously wrote that 'the glory of God is a human being fully alive and the life of a human being is the vision of God'.[11]

We are made for God and are only fully alive when moving towards that goal. This is not without struggles – purifications – as we cling so readily to all that is less than God, including our own wills. But the monk on the twelfth rung of the ladder of humility shows that the Holy Spirit, with our co-operation, can advance inner purification.

Lent is God's gift to help us focus on this task of accessing the astounding gift Christ has won for us through his Passion and resurrection. 'No one has ever seen God, it is the only Son, he who rests in the bosom of the Father, who has made him known' (John 1.18), or, as St Peter wrote: 'Christ died . . . the upright one, for the sake of the guilty, to lead us to God' (1 Pet. 3.18, my translations). So although a short chapter, RB 20 offers a succinct summary of the whole Christian/monastic journey of prayer through the process of purification of heart into a deeper union with God. Chapters 5–7 of the Rule give a more detailed picture of what is involved in this process of purification.

A mini treatise on prayer

The components of the triad – 'obedience' (RB 5), 'silence' or, as we've seen, more accurately 'restraint of speech' (RB 6), and 'humility' (RB 7) – are closely interrelated, any one of them leading to and, in a way, necessitating the others. When our hearts are humble, that is, not full of the clamorous ego-self, they are more receptive, more open to listen, to obey. Or we can start with the middle term of the triad, 'silence/restraint of speech', which clearly aids listening.

At first, when we pray, we shall probably hear our own distractedness and lack of ability to listen, our own lack of inner silence. This is humbling, this is true, and, since the truth sets us free (John 8.32), if we can only stay with that truth in humility, it will draw more of the light of truth into our hearts. Little by little, the Truth, Christ, through the Holy Spirit, purifies our hearts, stills them and begins to fill them with his peaceful, unifying presence.

So inasmuch as chapters 5–7 of the Rule mirror the dynamic of prayer, they help us to chart the inner journey. As ever, the life of Jesus is our model, he who:

> in the days of his flesh, offered up prayers and supplications to the one who was able to save him from death, and he was heard because of his reverent submission. Son though he was, he learned obedience through what he experienced, and having been made perfect, he became the source of eternal salvation for all who obey him.
> (Heb. 5.7–9, my translation)

Some translations have 'he learned obedience through what he suffered'. This is correct as long as we remember that 'to suffer' means 'to undergo', 'to experience', and so is not simply about 'suffering' and all that that conjures up about pain and difficulties. This line of thinking can end up exalting suffering per se as something good. Jesus came to take away our suffering – not with a swish of a baton but by undergoing and transforming it – and to empower us, through the Holy Spirit, to do the same.

We can see here a pattern similar to that in RB 5–7: obedience – listening to events in our lives; silence – taking them to prayer; humility – accepting them in trust that everything that happens to us occurs under the Father's loving gaze.

As followers of Christ, we are drawn into the same sequence, which operates on many scales, from having to come to terms with a serious illness to overcoming the need to have our own way in quite trivial matters. By 'clocking' our resistance while maintaining the desire to yield to God's will, and taking that honestly to prayer, we open ourselves to the Holy Spirit who can work to soften the most unyielding heart. Every encounter with the God who is truth will lead us deeper into humility. So from 'obedience', that is to say, from attentiveness even to our resistance to obeying God's will, through the silence of prayer, we grow in humility, that self-emptying that allows the Holy Spirit to fill us more fully. Yet it would be unhelpful to think that we must have totally mastered our passions and be perfectly recollected before we can pray! A hymn for the feasts of Saints Martha, Mary and Lazarus suggests that 'attentive stillness' flows from Christ's presence in our hearts in prayer:

> Christ Jesus to this house
> Come in, a welcome guest;
> Cast out our busy thoughts,
> Make space where you may rest.
> Grant us the peace that brings
> Attentive stillness, Lord;
> With quiet mind and heart
> May we receive your word.

> (Lauds hymn for the Feast of Saints Martha, Mary
> and Lazarus, 29 July, © Stanbrook Abbey)

The only real precondition for prayer is a desire to grow closer to God, a willingness to be open to receive, an acknowledgement of our neediness, a discernment of that 'one thing necessary' for our flourishing and from which all else will flow.

Blessings of attentiveness

The great blessing of attentiveness has to be that through it we grow closer to God. Prayer begins when we are attentive to the pull towards God that he has placed in our hearts. When we heed that call, and start to respond by deciding to commit time to personal prayer, we grow in self-knowledge. With this knowledge, there usually comes a realization that we need to change – *metanoia* – and the grace to do so is never lacking if we ask, so conversion can be seen as a further blessing of attentiveness. Gradually, through faithfulness in prayer, a kind of spiritual transfusion takes place as our more negative drives are overtaken by the fruits of the Holy Spirit: love, joy, peace, patience, kindness, gentleness, humility and self-control (Gal. 5.22–23). There are many regressions, of course, and any 'improvement' may be fairly imperceptible, but a sign that we are growing closer to God in prayer is that we are generally more accepting of our own and other people's shortcomings.

Then, like the monk on the twelfth rung of the ladder of humility, we may notice ourselves accomplishing life's challenges with less effort, whether it be strimming the lawn or loving a difficult neighbour. We are less easily thrown off course or upset, as hearts on the way to purification become more stable, more established in God's perfect love, which casts out fear (RB 7:67). We begin to be reintegrated interiorly.

A senior nun in our community, when speaking of prayer, used to describe a toy she had when a child. It seemed to be some sort of roundabout of dolls with many strings attached. The dolls were floppy and limp but when you tugged one central string, they sprang to life. So it is with prayer, which alone has the capacity to pull all the various, often tangled, strands of our life into a unity as we become more at one with God, ourselves, our neighbour and the whole cosmos.

A final thought: when we begin to grow in stability of heart we also grow in awareness of God's attentiveness to *us*, to the God who, in the words of John Henry Newman:

> beholds you individually, whoever you are. He 'calls you by name'. He sees you and understands you, because he made you . . . He views you in your day of rejoicing and your day of sorrow. He sympathizes in your hopes and your temptations . . . You are redeemed and sanctified, his adopted child, favoured with a portion of that glory and blessedness which flows from him . . . What is man, what are we, what am I, that the Son of God should be so mindful of me?[12]

For reflection and action

1

When all DESIRE

all EFFORT

all INCLINATION

all our THOUGHT

all that we LIVE

that we SPEAK

that we breathe

will be

G O D

And that unity which now is the Father's with the Son and the Son's with the Father will be poured into our perception and our mind so that, just as God loves us with sincere, pure and indissoluble love, we may be bound to God with perpetual and inseparable love, joined to him in such a way that

Whatever we BREATHE
whatever we KNOW
whatever we SPEAK
would be

G O D.

(St John Cassian, *Conference* X, VII, I)

2 Think about resolving (or re-resolving) to spend a definite amount of time daily in silent prayer. Be realistic: ten minutes daily is generally more beneficial than an hour sporadically.

3 Read something on prayer. You may like to choose Romans 8 or Luke's Gospel, focusing on how Jesus prays. The medieval classic, *The Cloud of Unknowing*, is short and readable. Cassian's *Conferences* IX and X may be found in English at <www.newadvent.org/fathers/3508.htm>.

4

The blessing of the Word

Listen readily to divine readings.
(RB 4:55)

The Word of God holds together the Rule like the strong vertical threads that form the warp of a piece of cloth and without which everything falls apart.

We shall look at St Benedict's use of Scripture in the Rule and consider some of the hurdles we face today in incorporating that Word into our lives. In the second part of the chapter we shall take the book of Baruch as an example of *lectio divina* to highlight some of the blessings of engaging with the Word.

In her award-winning autobiography, *True to Both My Selves*,[1] Katrin Fitzherbert recounts how her grandparents escaped on foot from Berlin before the advancing Red Army in April 1945. The author was convinced that it was her grandparents' 'intimate acquaintance' with Dickens's *David Copperfield*, particularly David's hazardous tramp from London to Dover, that had prepared them for their own ordeal. The story had become so much part of their lives that, in a sense, it enabled them to act. For me, this vignette captures something of the role of Scripture in the Benedictine way to God.

This chapter departs from the pattern adopted so far of following the Rule, unfolding in sequence, but we are by no means making a detour. Rather, we are drilling down to the bedrock that underlies the whole Rule and the whole of reality: 'In the beginning was the Word, and the Word was with God, and the Word was God . . . All things came into being through him, and without him not one thing came into being' (John 1.1, 3).

First, we need to explore the links between the 'Word' and 'Scripture'.

The Word of God and Scripture

Through his Word, God has communicated with us in a way we can understand. In this, St John Chrysostom (347–407) recognized the marvellous humility and loving-kindness of God in 'accommodating his language to our nature'.[2]

Although Jesus never speaks of himself as 'the Word', that is how some of his followers came to think of him when they reflected on their experience after his resurrection. We can hear the writer of St John's first letter grappling with this mysterious person they had known and loved, and wanting to share that experience with others:

> Something which has existed since the
>   beginning,
> which we have heard,
> which we have seen with our own eyes,
> which we have watched
> and touched with our own hands,
> the Word of life –
> this is our theme.
> That life was made visible;
> we saw it and are giving our testimony.
> (1 John 1.1–2, NJB)

48

Soon after John's time, St Irenaeus took up this identification of Christ with the Word. Commenting on Matthew 12.29, Irenaeus writes: 'God . . . took pity on the work modelled by his own hands, and granted salvation through the Word, that is, through Christ.'[3]

St Augustine was one of the early Christian writers who saw that God has spoken only one Word, his Son, who speaks throughout the Scriptures.[4] He perceived that the New Testament was hidden in the Old and the Old revealed in the New.[5]

The risen Christ, with the New Testament in the making, had pointed out as much to the disciples on the road to Emmaus, explaining to them all the parts of the Law and the Prophets that were about himself (Luke 24.27).

Benedict is in the tradition of such early Christian writers who used the terms 'the Word' and 'the Scriptures' virtually interchangeably.

So the Word has many manifestations, which include creation, the Scriptures, written and proclaimed, and the preaching of the gospel. We could say that the Scriptures form a subset of the Word or that the Word includes the Scriptures without being confined to them.

Christianity is therefore not a religion of the book but a religion of the Word, the Second Person of the blessed Trinity. Certain things follow when we consider the Word in this way. It means, first of all, that our contact with the Word of God is personal, and so *lectio divina* is more like prayer than an intellectual activity, though study of the Scriptures will enrich our *lectio divina*.

It also means that our contact with the Word is far broader than the time we devote to personal reading of the Bible, and includes hearing the readings proclaimed in church, 'reading' the book of nature and pondering the story of God's salvation in our own lives.

The Word in the Rule of St Benedict

The Scriptures rouse us . . .
(RB Prol. 8)

The image of being saturated by a story with which this chapter began would certainly have applied to anyone entering Benedict's monastery. From day one the aspiring monk would be exposed to the Word of God in Scripture (RB 53:9). Once showing a definite interest in becoming a monk, he would have the whole Rule, replete with scriptural references, read to him. On entering the monastery officially, he would be plunged into the story of salvation as recounted in the Bible, via the seven daily services and the nightly Vigils, where he would sing psalms and listen to and recite readings. His day would include lengthy periods of reading the Bible and committing passages to memory (RB 8:3). There would be reading at meals, no doubt from Scripture and scriptural commentaries, and the community would gather each evening before Compline to listen to one of the brothers reading aloud (RB 42:3–4). He would also hear the Rule itself read aloud 'often' in the monastery (RB 66:8). While, physically, the monks lived within the walls of the monastery, in a very real way they inhabited the Word.

The approach to the Word outlined above, sometimes called 'patristic', from its link with the early fathers of the Church, would have been that which prevailed in Benedict's time. 'Listen readily to divine readings' is one of the tools of good works (RB 4:55). While this indicates the more oral/aural culture of Benedict's time, it also reflects the early church approach to the Word perceived as a person discussed above.[6]

So, in the Rule, Scripture often addresses us directly: it 'shouts to us' at the start of RB 7; tells us to turn away from our own will (v. 19); teaches us (v. 25); exhorts us to hope in the Lord (v. 45); and shows us the pitfalls of too much talking (v. 57) – as well as addressing us directly through a handful of other references in RB 7 alone.[7]

Elsewhere, it is the 'voice of the Lord' that speaks, encouraging us through the words of Psalm 95/94 not to harden our hearts (RB Prol. 9–10), and, in RB 7:32, through the gospel, to imitate the Lord who came not to do his own will (John 6.38).

We saw in Chapter 2 of this book how the Rule exhorts us to follow the gospel as our guide. In RB 73:3, Benedict describes the whole of Scripture, both Old and New Testaments, as 'the truest of guides for human life'. Far from being contradictory, these two statements show the same approach to Scripture as the living Word of God, active throughout salvation history.

While it is difficult for us to attain this degree of immersion in the Word, given among other factors the exponential growth over the past millennium and a half of other words and media bombarding us from all sides, it should still be the aim of Christians to become 'inhabitants of the Bible rather than tourists in it',[8] for this is what Jesus has asked us to do and what will bring us freedom: 'If you abide in my word, you will indeed be my disciples; you will come to know the truth and the truth will set you free' (John 8.31–32, my translation).

In chapter 15 of John's Gospel, Jesus uses the image of the vine and its branches to illustrate the intimacy of this call to allow the sap of his Word – himself – to flow through us. If we abide in the Word, we are told that God will abide in us. We are driven by what fills our hearts, so this saturation of the heart by the Word will bring forth good fruit, will enable us to be one with the mind of Christ Jesus (see Phil. 2.5). This is the aim of all our contact with the Word in Scripture.

It sometimes surprises people that there is no chapter on *lectio divina* in the Rule of Benedict, but perhaps by now we can begin to see a wider pattern at work in the Rule concerning contact with the Word. The subject of the monks' reading comes up predominantly in RB 48, on 'Daily Manual Labour'; that is, in the context of work. For many monks this labour would have involved, first of all, learning to read, then the lifelong labour of working the Word into their lives.

While there are many differences between the respective challenges faced by monks in the sixth century and readers in the twenty-first century, at the level of the heart there is probably more common ground than we might think. The distractedness that we discussed in Chapter 3 will also tend to surface in our attempts to engage prayerfully with Scripture. However, the Desert Fathers came to recognize that in Scripture they had a powerful weapon to tame the demons of unruly thoughts; or again, they saw Scripture as a medicine that could heal the ills of the soul (RB 28:3).

John Cassian understood that while humans are powerless to stop the mind turning like a mill wheel, we can, with God's help, affect what goes into the mill. By rejecting harmful thoughts and filling the mind with Scripture, the heart becomes gradually more unified and purified.[9] He recommended short verses of Scripture, especially the Psalms, which could be used as arrow prayers in time of temptation. For example:

O God, come to my assistance;
O LORD, make haste to help me!
(Ps 70/69.1).[10]

We undoubtedly struggle today, often even within the monastery, to find that sense of spaciousness that abounds in the Rule. A favourite word for Benedict in writing about reading is *vacare* – the monks are to 'be free' for reading for what seems like a luxurious amount of time to us. But there is no point in wringing our hands about the pace of modern life. We have to do what we can and search our conscience about how we use the time at our disposal. And while we do have extra barriers to overcome in finding space for *lectio*, our technological age also provides many aids to the process of immersion: portable computers and media players, powerful search engines and online concordances, so for many in our culture, access to the Bible 24/7 is a possibility.

Lectio divina: simply reading, yet more than simply reading

Nothing can replace the slow, careful reading in silence that we would give to any serious reading. For before it is *lectio divina*, it is *lectio* – simply reading. Still, before we can engage with any text, there may be barriers to overcome. One might be the removal of any prejudice of the 'I don't like poetry' sort. As with most things, desire is more than half the battle. If you really want to read the great Russian novels, you are prepared to overcome the hurdle of those long names. So that same openness to the text and a willingness to lose oneself in reading that we bring to great literature are helpful attitudes in reading Scripture, much of which, before it can become our home, can often seem like a foreign country.

But it is also *lectio divina*, inspired by the same Holy Spirit we have as a gift from our baptism and that will enable us to detect the voice of Christ the Word through the words on the page or proclaimed. Probably the key disposition we need to bring to our *lectio* is faith.

As Dietrich Bonhoeffer wrote in 1938, in a passage that captures the essence of *lectio divina*:

> We ponder the chosen text on the strength of the promise that it has something utterly personal to say for us . . . We do not ask what the text has to say to other people . . . We are not expounding [the text] or preparing a sermon or conducting a Bible study; we are rather waiting for God's Word to us. It is not a vacuous waiting but a waiting on the basis of a clear promise. Often we are so burdened and overwhelmed with other thoughts, images and concerns that it may take a long time before God's Word has swept all else aside and come through. But it will surely come, just as surely as God himself has come and will come again. This is the very reason why we begin . . . with the prayer that God may send his Holy Spirit to us through his Word and reveal his Word to enlighten us.[11]

It is to such personal *lectio divina* that we turn for the second part of this chapter.

Lectio divina with the book of Baruch

Chapter 48 of the Rule provides a window into the Lenten reading of the monks in Benedict's monastery and may help us with our own reading:

In these days of Lent, let them each receive a book from the library, which they shall read straight through and entirely (*per ordinem ex integro*); let these books be distributed at the beginning of Lent.[12]
(RB 48:15–16)

The phrase 'straight through and entirely' is just about the sum total of Benedict's instructions on how to 'do' *lectio divina*! It's not clear whether this was to be the monks' practice at all times or whether it was one of the ways they were 'to wash away, during these holy days, the negligence of other times' (RB 49:3). At any rate, it suggests Benedict was aware of the butterfly tendencies to which humans can be prone in their reading habits. While any contact with the Word is to be encouraged, and is certainly beneficial, we miss out on a great deal if we are continually 'cherry-picking' our favourite passages from the Bible.

We need to be challenged by the Word as well as comforted. Like prayer, Scripture acts as a mirror (Jas. 1.22–25) and has the power to purify our hearts (John 15.3), to unify them, and so to transform us. But to receive the fullness of these blessings we need, at least sometimes, to grapple with a whole text, even and especially with the parts we find difficult. We need to be like Jacob, who struggled against that mysterious partner until he received a blessing (Gen. 32.22–32). In our encounters with the Word, there may be the occasional dramatic breakthrough in self-understanding, such as the one Jacob seems to have experienced. More often, though, it's a question of a gradual transformation by the action of the Holy Spirit into the image of Christ 'from one degree of glory to another' (2 Cor. 3.18). Either way, we shall be changed by opening our hearts to the whole message of Scripture. Cultivating the practice of reading whole books of the Bible, even if only during Lent, is very much part of the way to God that Benedict maps out.

In our monastery we continue this traditional Benedictine practice. On Ash Wednesday, each nun receives from the abbess a book of Scripture to ponder in depth during the weeks of Lent. Sometimes during Eastertide we share the fruits of this reading with one another. In that vein, I would like to share with you my experience of reading, a few Lents ago, the book of Baruch. This is not a commentary or a scholarly exegesis but simply a sharing of some reflections.

Preparation

Mindful that in *lectio divina* we are opening our hearts to the voice of the Lord as it speaks to us directly, we do not need to become experts in ancient languages and biblical studies before we can engage with a book of the Bible. Background knowledge is helpful but it can get in the way of *lectio* if we worry about details. Even so, it can be a useful exercise, especially when faced with a book of the Old Testament, simply to get one's bearings by looking up some background information.

On receiving the book of Baruch, I first took stock of what I already knew. I was familiar with a few passages that crop up in the liturgy, for example at the Easter Vigil, and I knew that 'Baruch' was the name of Jeremiah's secretary. So I assumed I would be reading one of the Prophetic books from about the sixth to seventh century BCE.

In fact, scholars consider the book to have been written in the first century before Christ, and so clearly it could not have been written by Jeremiah's secretary. It seems, rather, that the author was drawing on the tradition of the great prophet of the exile, Jeremiah, to help the Jews living an internal exile in their own land under the Greek Empire in the first century BCE. This discovery was heartening: if the story of the Babylonian exile of God's chosen people in the sixth century BCE could be used to encourage others living under a different kind of despotic regime 500 years later, then it might have something to say to anyone struggling with oppressive forces of any kind today.

I also discovered that the name 'Baruch' can be translated as 'Blessed'. Armed with this brief background, intrigued by the 'Blessed', and having prayed to the Holy Spirit, I set about reading. Since Baruch has only six chapters,[13] I decided to read the whole book through fairly quickly once, followed by a slow, prayerful read at *lectio* pace, and several rereadings during Lent.

Reflections on the text

With great economy, in the first 14 verses the author tells us that he wrote the words to be read aloud to the Jewish exiles in Babylon. He recounts how his audience wept, fasted and prayed on hearing the words, and were moved to send alms to their fellow countrymen in Jerusalem, together with a request for prayers. We learn that a scroll of what seems to be the same words of Baruch that they themselves have heard read aloud was also sent to the exiles' fellow countrymen still in Jerusalem.

It struck me that here was a cameo of Lent: Scripture, prayer, fasting, almsgiving, all flowing from that engagement with the Word in Scripture. This opening of Baruch called to mind other passages where we see the Word piercing the hearts of listeners and prompting them to act. There was John the Baptist's powerful preaching of a baptism of repentance using the words of the prophet Isaiah, which bore fruit in the conversion of many (see Luke 3.1–14). Later, in Acts, we read that those who heard Peter's Pentecost preaching of the resurrection of Christ 'were cut to the heart' and asked the Apostles 'what should we do?' (Acts 2.37). I was reminded of those words from Hebrews that 'the word of God is living and active' (Heb. 4.12) and I prayed to be open to that creative energy.

The book of Baruch then unfolds in four main movements:

1 compunction/confession
2 conversion
3 prayer
4 consolation.

With repeated reading and reflecting, I came to see not simply the narrative of what happened in this story but also a model of what often happens when we engage with the Word in *lectio divina*. But we need to be aware of the danger of any model that sets out stages in the spiritual life. While they can be helpful as descriptions of what can happen, if used to assess 'where we are', they tend to shift our focus away from God so we become unstuck, rather like trying to learn to ride a bicycle with a manual in one hand. The medieval fourfold pattern of *lectio divina* as *lectio* (reading), *meditatio* (ruminating), *oratio* (praying) and *contemplatio* (contemplating), outlined by Guigo II in his *Ladder for Monks*, is a case in point.[14]

1 Compunction/confession

Much of the first half of the book of Baruch is made up of a heart-rending, stunningly honest confession to God that the people have not listened to his voice. This is what Baruch implies was on the scroll that was sent to be read out in Jerusalem:

The Lord our God is in the right, but there is open shame
on us today . . . [because] . . . we have sinned before the
Lord. We have disobeyed him, and have not heeded the
voice of the Lord our God, to walk in the statutes of the
Lord that he set before us . . . we have been negligent, in
not heeding his voice.
(Bar. 1.15, 17–19)

Variations on this confession appear a further seven times
in the first three chapters of the book.[15] Here, the import of
Benedict's admonition that the whole text should be read
becomes clear: faced with such massive repetition, it is hard to
escape looking into one's own conscience for negligence and to
admit that one has not always listened to God.

2 Conversion

In response to this humble confession, Baruch brings in the
voice of the Lord, ever ready to renew his covenant with his
people:

In the land of their exile they will come to themselves
and know that I am the Lord their God. I will give them a
heart that obeys and ears that hear; they will praise me in
the land of their exile, and will remember my name and
turn from their stubbornness and their wicked deeds.
(Bar. 2.30–33)

The story of the Prodigal Son, who 'came to himself' in his
distress working on the pig farm away from his father's house
(Luke 15.15–17), entered my mind as I read this text, and I
reflected again on the Prologue to the Rule of St Benedict, with

its echoes of the Prodigal's story and my own journey back to
God through the monastic life. It was a moment to draw grace
again from that conversion, to give thanks and to pray for a
deepening of the self-knowledge that tells me, though a sinner,
I am God's beloved daughter and that he is always awaiting
my return.

3 Prayer: an appeal for mercy

Overlapping with this confession and arising spontaneously
out of it comes further prayer for God's mercy: 'The soul in
anguish and the wearied spirit cry out to you. Hear, O Lord,
and have mercy, for we have sinned before you' (Bar. 3.1–2).
These words echo those in the liturgy for Ash Wednesday and
can be used as an 'arrow prayer', of the kind used by the Desert
Fathers, at any time.

4 Consolation

Take courage, my children, cry to God,
and he will deliver you from the power and
    hand of the enemy.
For I have put my hope in the Everlasting to
    save you,
and joy has come to me from the Holy One,
because of the mercy that will soon come to
    you
from your everlasting saviour.
For I sent you out with sorrow and weeping,
but God will give you back to me with joy and
    gladness for ever.
(Bar. 4.21–23)

A personified Jerusalem is the original voice here, but how well it fits as a prayer for anyone parted from loved ones in any age.

Twice more in chapter 4 'Take courage!' rings out. In verses 27–29, Jerusalem continues to speak:

> Take courage, my children, and cry to God . . .
> For just as you were disposed to go astray
>   from God,
> return with tenfold zeal to seek him.
> (Bar. 4.27–28)

But in verse 30, suddenly the voice of the Lord breaks through:

> Take courage, O Jerusalem,
> for the one who named you will comfort you.
> (Bar. 4.30)

For the early Christian writers, 'Jerusalem' was often read as a symbol of the individual soul. Despite all the lack of listening and the negligence on our part, God never takes back his gifts nor revokes his choice (see Rom. 11.29). I thanked God for my baptism and vocation.

As Easter drew closer, this chapter of Baruch with its three-fold call to 'take courage' brought to mind that same phrase put on the lips of Jesus at the Last Supper in John's Gospel. Night has fallen, Judas has gone out and the sense of evil closing in on Jesus is palpable:

> The hour is coming, indeed it has come, when you will be scattered, each one to his home, and you will leave

me alone. Yet I am not alone because the Father is with me. I have said this to you, so that in me you may have peace. In the world you face persecution. But take courage; I have conquered the world!
(John 16.32–33)

This Lenten reading had taken me to the joy of the resurrection. Each strand of Scripture will do the same if we read in the light of the Risen Christ.

The blessings of the Word

And what about the name 'Baruch'? In what might the blessedness implied in the name consist? One answer might come from the text itself, 'blessed are we: what pleases God has been revealed to us' (Bar. 4.4, njb). The blessedness of Israel is in keeping the Lord's commandments as revealed through Moses. Baruch's blessedness seems to be linked with his calling back Israel to this revelation of the Lord in the sacred Scriptures. For Christians, this revelation has been crystallized in Christ, God's revelation to us of himself. Mary of Nazareth was called blessed for believing the message that she would give birth to God's Son, the Word incarnate (Luke 1.45). Yet, astonishingly, Luke's Gospel later ascribes an even greater blessedness to those – surely including Mary of Nazareth in the first place – 'who hear the word of God and obey it' (Luke 11.28).

This means us! And the way of Benedict, so centred on the Word of God, is a trusty path for those who follow it to grow in that beatitude.

For reflection and action

Lord, may your Word ever be the guiding light of our
lives and the source of our peace.
(Based on the Collect for the Feast of St Pachomius,
a founder of the monastic life, 15 May, Stanbrook
translation)

1 Personally, or in a group, select or receive a book of the
  Bible to read during Lent. During Eastertide, you may wish
  to meet and share the fruits of your reading.
2 Adopt a resting and rising prayer from the Psalms.
  For example:

  I lie down, I sleep and I wake,
  for the LORD upholds me.
  (Ps. 3.6)

  Psalm 139/138 offers scope for other prayers.
3 Meditation on the Word of God:

  Why is he spoken of as 'Word'? Because, when he sounded
  his voice, he awakened all creatures and called them to
  himself . . .
     Without the Word of God, no creature exists, because
  through the Word of God, every creature, visible and
  invisible, was created in which subsists the living Spirit,
  or 'viriditas' or strength.[16]
  (St Hildegard of Bingen, 1098–1179)

5

The blessing of worship: RB 8–20

The Prophet says: *Seven times a day I have praised you.*
(RB 16:1)

The story so far . . .

Benedict first gives us the inspiring Prologue, which sets out the goal of the journey: eternal life. Then, over the course of the first seven chapters, he situates this journey within the context of a community following the gospel precepts of love of God and neighbour, and lays down the spiritual foundations needed to advance towards our goal of eternal life with God: obedience, humility and a degree of silence to foster *lectio divina* and prayer.

From RB 8 onwards we see the working of this inner spirit manifested in more outward 'works': worship of God; reverent attention towards neighbour, self and the material world; and hospitality. These form the subjects of the next three chapters in this book.

Lent and monastic life: turning back to God

[to] bring you back to him from whom you had strayed . . .
(Prol. 2)

Liturgical prayer, for which the community gathers several times a day and sometimes at night to praise God, is perhaps the defining characteristic of Benedictines. The ordered beauty of monastic worship seems to help people to sense the transcendent, and many who have never set foot inside a monastery appreciate Gregorian chant. In worship we turn back to our Creator, align ourselves once more with the light of God's face revealed to us in Christ.

As we shall see below, this emphasis on worship is clear in the Rule but undoubtedly has a broader context deeply rooted in the human psyche. Monuments such as the Pyramids of Egypt, Stonehenge and the many prehistoric burial sites that are to be found across the British landscape, attest to a profoundly religious spirit in our ancestors. Even today, while church attendance in the West is falling, the spontaneous public outpouring of grief in response to national or local disasters, expressed for example in candlelit vigils, flowers at the site of the tragedy and hashtags identifying with the victims, all surely spring from that same inner impulse to ritualize our emotions. *Homo sapiens* may perhaps more accurately be described as *Homo religiosus*.

The priority of worship in the Rule of St Benedict

Let nothing be put before the Work of God.
(RB 43:3)

Chapters 8–20 of the Rule, often called the Liturgical Code, offer a detailed description of the regime of worship in Benedict's monastery. There is no preamble, no introduction on the theology of liturgy; instead, we are plunged, as the newcomer to the monastery would have been, into the round of community prayer:

> In winter, that is from 1 November until Easter, the brethren shall rise at the eighth hour of the night, so that they may sleep a little beyond midnight and rise with their digestion completed.
> (RB 8:1)

The service of Vigils that followed comprised 14 psalms, a hymn, four scriptural or patristic readings with responses,[1] a Scripture verse and the litany; that is, 'Lord, have mercy'. It began, as the first office in Benedictine monasteries today begins, with 'O Lord, open my lips/ and my mouth shall proclaim your praise' (Ps. 51/50.17).

By the time the monk returns to bed in the evening of the same day, he will have taken part in seven more services: Lauds, Prime, Terce, Sext, None, Vespers and Compline, spread throughout the day, and on some days will also have attended the Eucharist.

These chapters are for the most part instructions about the timing and composition of the various services or 'offices' – there is even one chapter solely on when 'alleluia' should be said – but we are not simply dealing with rubrics. It would be difficult to overestimate the importance of community worship in Benedict's Rule. The amount of time (about three to four hours a day) devoted to corporate prayer backs up this assertion. Zeal for the Work of God is the first criterion to be looked for in discerning the authenticity of a novice's calling (RB 58:7).

Significant, too, are the editorial changes Benedict has made from his immediate source, the Rule of the Master. First,

Benedict has made a tighter, more unified unit of the chapters on the liturgy than is found in the Rule of the Master; then he has moved the whole unit much closer to the start of the Rule, so that it becomes the first, and longest, piece of extended teaching after the spiritual chapters on obedience, silence and humility.

Benedict legislated that each night at Vigils, after the brief introductory Psalm 3, Psalm 95/94 should be chanted right through. Even today this is still called the Invitatory Psalm as it invites the assembly to worship:

> O come; let us bow and bend low.
> Let us kneel before the God who made us,
> for he is our God and we the people,
> the people of his pasture.
> (Ps. 95/94.6–7)

That's it in a nutshell. Benedict's whole approach to the life of worship in his monastery flows from this and matches what he states should be the priority for the monks on hearing the bell for church: 'nothing is to be put before the Work of God' (RB 43:3).

Is the Liturgical Code relevant for Christians in the world?

Some might say 'no', consigning chapters 8–20 to an appendix for a lay audience. If we stay at the surface level of how the Work of God was performed in Benedict's monastery 1,500 years ago, then it is easy to dismiss these chapters as being of limited relevance to people trying to live a faithful Christian life in the world, few of whom will have time or inclination to chant 150 psalms a week. But when we gaze steadily into the depths of the great sea of psalmody, I think it is possible to detect two strong currents that drive these chapters on worship and flow through the lives of all Christians. The first is the centrality of Easter; the second, our Judaeo-Christian patrimony, particularly as expressed in the psalms.

The centrality of Easter

Looking forward with joy and spiritual longing to the holy feast of Easter.
(see RB 49:7)

In Chapter 2 we explored the Rule as a guide to the gospel, the good news that Christ is risen. So Lent for Benedict is above all a time of looking forward to Easter. The whole Rule is marked by this paschal expectation. Everything in the monastery, from the times and character of services and meal times to the arrangement of work and reading, revolves around that pivotal point. In this way, the Passion, death, resurrection and ascension of Christ, known together as his 'paschal mystery', become thoroughly worked into the life of a monk or nun or anyone who follows Benedict's way closely.

Concrete examples of Benedict's emphasis on Easter include his wish that the weekly cycle always begin anew on Sunday (RB 18:23), the day of the resurrection. Similarly, we note that he styles the office of Lauds on Sundays throughout the year a 'solemnity' (RB 12), a title otherwise reserved for the major liturgical celebrations like Easter and Pentecost. We have already mentioned that there is a whole chapter (RB 15) setting out when the exclamation most associated with Easter, 'alleluia', may be said.[2]

Further, Easter shapes the rest of the liturgical year. In churches of the Catholic/Apostolic tradition in the West, different colours match the various liturgical seasons, and are used, for example, for the vestments of the clergy and altar frontals. The white/gold of Easter is preceded by the six weeks of Lent and its purple hues, followed by the 50 days of Paschaltide culminating in the red of Pentecost to denote the descent of the Holy Spirit who brings life. It is no coincidence that the time following Pentecost is marked in the liturgical calendar by the green of new life. These liturgical colours coordinate with the readings, hymns and melodies that are in harmony with the mood of the season: more sombre, reflective and penitential in Lent, giving way to the joyful explosion of alleluias at Eastertide. Gradually these liturgical seasons come to colour the lives of those who live them. In northern latitudes, the liturgical seasons often chime in with the natural seasons; for example, the word 'Lent' is derived from the 'lengthening' of daylight hours experienced in the northern latitudes. But they also override the prevailing natural conditions. Think how the joyful expectation of the Advent liturgy lightens the darkness of a northern December.

In short, the Easter focus of worship in the Rule heightens an awareness of, and faith in, the resurrection and so deepens our Christian faith. Little by little, the life and light of Christ, held and conveyed in the liturgy, pervade the lives of those who open themselves to this form of his presence, and then spill out into the rest of life.

Judaeo-Christian patrimony

Monotheistic worship was the characteristic mark of the chosen people of Israel in which our Christian faith is rooted.

Codified in the Ten Commandments (Exod. 20.1–17), this worshipping of the one Lord can be traced back to Noah, who built an altar to sacrifice to the Lord after the Flood (Gen. 8.20), then on through Abraham's sacrifices (Gen. 15.1–21; 22.1–19) and Jacob's vow (Gen. 28.20–22). At the Exodus, it was the urgent need for the captive people of Israel to worship the Lord in the wilderness that was at the heart of Moses' pleas to Pharaoh for their release.

'Then the LORD said to Moses: "Go to Pharaoh and say to him, 'Thus says the LORD: Let my people go, so that they may worship me'"' (Exod. 8.1). This is not the sycophantic worship demanded by a despotic magnate but the human side of that covenant relationship, marked on God's side by steadfast love and mercy.

Owing to lack of sources, it is difficult to speak with any precision about the patterns and content of the services of worship of the earliest Christians.[3] By the second century, there are references in patristic writings to prayer at dawn, then at the third, sixth and ninth hours, as well as in the evening and at night. Some traditions link these to specific 'hours' of Christ's Passion as found in the gospel narratives, for example his arrest at the third hour (9 a.m.), crucifixion at the sixth hour (noon) and death at the ninth hour (3 p.m.), while the dawn service commemorates the hour of the resurrection and the nightly vigil is in expectation of the last coming.[4] But it is surely not fanciful to think there would have been some continuity between Jewish patterns of daily prayer and those that developed in Christianity. In the New Testament we read how the first followers of Christ kept up their daily attendance at the Temple in Jerusalem (Acts 2.46), and a little later we find Peter and John on their way up to the Temple around 3 p.m. for the afternoon hour of prayer (Acts 3.1).

Psalms would almost certainly have formed the bedrock of such services, as they do in the liturgical code of Benedict's Rule.[5] As we saw in Chapter 1, Benedict, in editing his nearest source, the Rule of the Master, chose to include in his own Rule those sections that were rich in psalms. As powerful prayers of supplication and thanksgiving, they open the heart to receive God's transforming grace. They unite us to the great story of God's redemption of his people. The psalms, like the whole of the liturgy of which they form the backbone, are one great act of remembrance or of corporate mindfulness. As such, they distil many of the blessings outlined in Chapters 1, 3 and 4 above as channels of communication between God and the human heart.

But we need to experience the power of the psalms and prayers rather than simply read about them. Programme notes are no substitute for the actual performance of any work. The office of Lauds begins each day with Psalm 67/66, a short psalm printed in full here:

> May God be gracious to us and bless us!
> May he let his face shine upon us
> and show us his mercy,
> so that we may know his way on earth
> and that all nations may know your salvation.
> Let the peoples praise you, O God;
> let all the peoples praise you!
> Let the nations be glad and exult,
> for you judge the peoples fairly
> and guide the peoples on earth.
> Let the peoples praise you O God;
> let all the peoples praise you!
> The earth has given its fruit.

May God, our God, bless us!
May God give us his blessing,
and let all the ends of the earth revere him!
(Ps. 67/66, my translation from the Vulgate)

In its original Jewish context, this psalm was one of thanks-giving for the blessing of a good harvest. A Christian reading of it sees Christ as the harvest blessing; he who died and rose from the earth. Benedict wishes his community to sing the psalm at the very start of the office of Lauds at daybreak, the daily remembrance of the Lord's resurrection: 'The earth has given its fruit.' One can imagine the impact of these words chanted as the new light of day was breaking on a world without electricity. Even today, in those monasteries that have retained Benedict's arrangement of the psalms, this one rings out as a powerful summons to praise, quietly triumphant and full of gratitude.

The same three psalms – Psalms 4; 91/90; 134/133 – were sung each night in Benedict's monastery. It is not difficult to see a reason for the inclusion of Psalm 4 at the end of the day:

'O that we might see better times,' many say.
Lift up the light of your face on us, O LORD . . .
In peace I will lie down and fall asleep,
for you alone, O LORD, make me dwell in safety.
(Ps. 4.7, 9)

Psalm 91/90, a longer psalm of confidence in God's power and protection against the forces of darkness, is used extensively in the Church's liturgy for Lent. The lines, 'he will conceal you with his pinions/and under his wings you will find refuge'

(Ps. 91/90.4), resonate with Jesus' time of temptation of 40 days in the desert after which Lent is patterned. The whole psalm makes a powerful meditation for Lent, which you may like to consider incorporating into your daily prayer schedule.

Psalm 134/133 is a summons to praise that mirrors the opening psalm at Vigils (Ps. 95/94). Thus the Benedictine day is bookended with praise:

> O come, bless the LORD,
> all you servants of the LORD,
> who stand by night in the courts
> of the house of the LORD.
> Lift up your hands to the holy place,
> and bless the LORD.
> (Ps. 134/133.1–2)

The Benedictus (Luke 1.68–79), sung at Lauds every day, unites the two currents we have been considering: the centrality of Easter and our Judaeo-Christian patrimony. Beginning with 'Blessed be the LORD', after the pattern of so many of the psalms, the aged Zechariah goes on to sing a birthday ode to his newborn son, John the Baptist, the herald of Christ at the dawn of salvation. It is a song full of hope made real by the inclusion of the darkness and enemies that the light of the gospel has come to dispel.

Summing up: gravity and reverence in RB 8–20

> As soon as the cantor has begun the 'Glory be to the Father', let all rise from their seats in honour and reverence to the Holy Trinity.
> (RB 9:7)

This section of the Rule is permeated by an aura of gravity and reverence. At the close of the Liturgical Code, Benedict offers some more general advice on the chanting of psalms, which calls the monks to that attentiveness of which we spoke in Chapter 3.

> We believe that God is present everywhere . . . but let us especially believe this when we are assisting at the Work of God . . . Let us therefore consider how we should behave in the presence of God and his angels and so stand to sing the psalms that mind and voice may be in harmony.
>
> (RB 19:1–2, 6–7)

While the detailed prescription of which psalms should be sung when is probably something of more concern to monastics or those committed to the recitation of the Divine Office, there is, I think, something for all Christians to ponder in Benedict's insistence on an attitude of awe in the presence of God. Our age has, at least in the West, largely lost a sense of the sacred both in terms of space and of time. Even in Christian communities there seems to be a tension between welcoming people and preserving a sense of reverence. Monasteries are known for their hospitality but also manage to keep the monastic church as a place of silence. It is true that they usually have the facilities for keeping these two activities of welcoming and prayer in discrete places, but at base it comes down to the ethos of the Rule in which Benedictine communities are steeped. Some parishes have been creative in thinking round this tension between welcoming and reverence. One parish I know is very good at greeting people on arrival, then, five minutes before the service is due to begin, a designated person welcomes the whole assembly and invites the congregation into silence to prepare themselves for what is about to take place in the liturgy.

In the end we are each responsible for establishing and maintaining a prayerful atmosphere in our place of worship. Lent is a good time to review this and to think about ways we can promote reverence both as communities and as individuals.

Some blessings of worship

First of all, worship, which for Christians is always accomplished 'in Christ', restores us to right relationship with God: creature to Creator. It undoes that mysterious refusal to serve and worship God that tradition sees as Lucifer's sin, rooted in pride, and that we perhaps recognize in ourselves whenever we say 'Why should I?', either in our service of God or neighbour made in God's image.

Worship nurtures in us that 'fear of the LORD', or reverence, which is the beginning of wisdom (Prov. 9.10). Benedict stresses this as the ground of humility (RB 7:10–30), which we saw in Chapter 3 leads to perfect love. As we are made for love, worship therefore helps us to attain our vocation as human beings.

By exhorting us to put nothing before worship of God, Benedict is recalling us to our freedom as humans made to be in right relationship with our Creator, a relationship marked by the freedom of love. But there is a caveat. The Lord's words to his chosen people, 'I desire steadfast love and not sacrifice' (Hos. 6.6), are for all people and all time, and Jesus himself reminds us that true worshippers are those who worship 'in spirit and truth' (John 4.24). Benedictines above all need to remember this to prevent the pitfalls of empty ritual.

While, as already mentioned, it is difficult for lay people – and not everyone's calling – to fit in eight full services daily, the regularity of a set pattern of stopping to worship God throughout the day is a Benedictine practice that can be adapted to everyone's situation. Freed from our whims and feelings, a regular pattern of daily worship – Benedict writes of the 'discipline' of psalmody (RB 19) – pays fitting homage to the God who never stops loving us, while simultaneously bringing blessings to every level of our being. Because the human being is a body–soul composite, fostering inner balance and peace through worship has a physical impact and can reduce stress levels.

Some people with families and jobs do manage to pray the whole Divine Office, while others pray Morning and Evening Prayer. But simply to recite prayerfully a psalm at the beginning, middle and end of the day, or a few key lines from a psalm or the Lord's Prayer, can be enough to inject some equilibrium into a frantic schedule. It is not so much the length of time spent in turning to God during the day as the fact of stopping and 'recalculating', reminding ourselves that God is our source and goal, all-powerful, our stay and protection throughout the day. Such a habit of turning to God at short, regular intervals helps to put whatever life throws at us into perspective. We shall develop this idea in Chapter 6.

The Anglican Divine, William Law (1686–1761), describes the great power of praise and thanksgiving to transform situations:

> If anyone would tell you the shortest, surest way to all happiness and all perfection, he must tell you to make a rule to yourself, to thank and praise God for

everything that happens to you. For it is certain that whatever seeming calamity happens to you, if you thank and praise God for it, you turn it into a blessing. Could you therefore work miracles, you could not do more for yourself than by this thankful spirit; for it heals with a word speaking, and turns all that it touches into happiness.[6]

Last, but not least, worship fosters in us a sense of reverence and alters our relationship to time, freeing us from its tyranny. To these we turn next.

For reflection and action

1 Personally, or in a group, ponder the Benedictus (Luke 1.68–79) as *lectio divina*.

2 Consider incorporating the Benedictus into your morning prayer.

3 During Lent you may like to experiment by adding some of the psalms recommended by St Benedict for morning and night prayer. For example, Psalm 67/66 for morning prayer and Psalm 91/90 for the evening/night. You could explore RB 8–20 to find more examples.

4 Consider attending a monastic office or service. *The Benedictine Year Book* has details of where monasteries are to be found in Britain, Ireland and overseas, or see <www.benedictine-oblates.net>.

5 Think about, and perhaps discuss in a group, how your worshipping community manages the tension between welcoming people and maintaining a reverent atmosphere.

6

The blessing of reverence: RB 20–52

All the utensils and property of the monastery should be regarded as sacred altar vessels.

(RB 31:10)

One of the striking features of the Rule of St Benedict is the way its ethos of reverence extends across all aspects of life in the monastery. There is no distinction between the 'sacred' and 'profane'; everyday pots and pans are to be treated with as much care as the most precious artefacts in the sacristy, for, as Benedict wrote at the end of the Liturgical Code, 'We believe that God is present everywhere' (RB 19:1). Whether it is a question of arranging work or fixing prices for goods made in the monastery, mindfulness of God should prevail and care be taken 'so that in all things God may be glorified' (RB 57:9).

In this chapter we consider how the reverential attitudes of the Rule towards human beings and material creation can be a blessing in our culture, so often marked by stress and a throwaway mentality. We shall take an overview of RB 20–52 to see how reverence is incarnated in the monastery, before looking more closely at one often neglected area: how the Rule can help us develop a more reverent approach to ourselves.

Overview: RB 20–52

> Teach me, my God and King,
> In all things thee to see,
> And what I do in any thing,
> To do it as for thee . . .
> A servant with this clause
> Makes drudgerie divine:
> Who sweeps a room, as for thy laws,
> Makes that and th' action fine.[1]

Herbert's poem encapsulates the Benedictine approach, which is nothing more nor less than the Christian one. The triune God created all things through his Word, and by entering that creation as Christ, the Word incarnate has, through Christ's death and resurrection, sent the Spirit, which is bringing the divine plan for creation to its goal of complete unity. This cosmic vision of reality, found in Scripture, for example in the opening chapter of the Letter to the Ephesians, reverberates through every atom of the created world. Nothing is outside its scope; everything matters, and Paul can write: 'whether you eat or drink, or whatever you do, do everything for the glory of God' (1 Cor. 10.31).

Such an approach, sometimes called incarnational or sacramental, pervades the Rule. One clear example of where the more obviously 'holy' and 'mundane' meet is seen in RB 35, on 'Weekly Kitchen Servers'. Those engaged in serving at meals receive a blessing in the oratory on Sunday and recite the very same verse which opens each monastic office:

> O God, come to my assistance;
> O LORD, make haste to help me!
> (Ps. 70/69.2)

The same verse is sung by the refectory reader of the week. Many monasteries today retain variations on these customs. In the home, grace before meals can be a powerful reminder of the sacredness of all aspects of life.

Chapters 20–52 of the Rule encompass large tracts of life: work, rest, the arrangements for meal times, the quality and quantity of food and drink, how it should be served and details about the reading that traditionally accompanies the monks' silent meals. There are chapters on the supply and care of the material goods of the monastery, care of the sick and the wayward.

We can think of this central section of the Rule as a vast canopy, suspended between the chapters on prayer (RB 20) and the oratory (RB 52), covering everything beneath it in an aura of reverence.

Much of the teaching about how the daily round in the monastery is to be carried comes via carefully drawn pen portraits of personnel: for example, RB 31, 'What sort of person the cellarer [bursar] should be'; or RB 36, on care of the sick, which reads as a job description of the infirmarian.

This speaks volumes about Benedict's attitude: people count. The most elaborate schemes and work targets are doomed to failure unless the people doing the jobs are engaged in the task with a sense of responsibility and worth.

'Let him take care of everything' (RB 31:3)

While competence is not insignificant and is specifically mentioned a little further on in the Rule for those in charge of the guest kitchen (RB 53:17), what stands out in this section is the care – reverence – that these daily tasks demand if people's needs are to be met on a human scale.

The word 'care' (Latin *cura*) crops up ten times in RB 20–52. There is the abbot's care for the wayward (RB 27:1) and the awareness he must have of the frailty of all those in his care (RB 27:6). The cellarer, under the authority of the abbot, is to take care of everything in the monastery (RB 31:3, 15), especially the needs of the most vulnerable, the sick, children, guests, the poor (RB 31:9). Unsurprisingly, RB 36, on care of the sick, has three mentions of *cura*. Delegated to the infirmarian, it is the responsibility of the abbot to ensure that the sick suffer no neglect. The other two instances concern the abbot's taking care that the times for the Divine Office are signalled faithfully (RB 47:1). Although at first this may seem to be different from caring for the people and goods of the monastery, it is really of a piece with these, as I hope will become clear.

The concept of 'taking care' of things has profound significance, for it reflects our role as stewards – curators – of God's creation. No act is without an impact where even the movement of a butterfly's wing registers throughout the universe; it matters how we handle things.

Perhaps a helpful way for lay people to read the disciplinary measures of RB 21–31 (see also 32:4–5) is to notice how often it is precisely care*lessness* that is challenged by the Rule, as this goes against that monastic ethos of attentiveness we considered in Chapter 3, which seeks to give glory to God in all things and to see Christ in all people (RB 36:1).

'We believe it will suffice . . . Let frugality be maintained in all things' (RB 39:1, 10)

If it matters how we treat things in a finite world, it also matters how much of anything we use. Taking seriously our ecological responsibilities involves some sort of personal asceticism.

These principles are embedded in the Rule. The 'frugality' is not parsimonious and perhaps can be seen more as 'simplicity'. The monks receive two square meals a day, with a variety of dishes and a generous pound of bread plus a measure of wine, extras being added when the abbot sees fit (RB 39 and 40).

The list of things that the monastery supplies for the monk was impressive (see RB 55) and is so today. We lack little in the monastery. What Benedict teaches is moderation, a fitting measure of food, drink or whatever. While those who live in the world cannot afford the luxury of having no personal purchasing power, what the Rule has to teach about discretion in what is consumed (in the broadest sense) and sharing resources is transferable to any life.

Each Lent, in many monasteries, monks and nuns are required to make a list for the superior's attention of the items they have for their own use. This can be a helpful way to keep personal 'stuff' from spiralling out of control.

But there's more. As well as our vocation as curators of God's creation, we are called by our baptism to share in Christ's priestly role as a median figure between God and the world. This concept, perhaps better developed in the Orthodox tradition, is also part of our Christian heritage in the West.[2]

'Priestly' here is not about the hierarchical, sacramental priesthood but rather sees the human being, on the one hand, acting as on God's behalf, charged with care for creation, and, on the other, offering up, as creation's voice, praise and thanks to God. As Peter wrote to the early Christians of Asia Minor: 'You are a chosen race, a royal priesthood, a holy nation, God's own people, in order that you may proclaim the mighty acts of him who called you out of darkness into his marvellous light' (1 Pet. 2.9).

The psalms resound with this reverent chorus of praise to the Creator for, and on behalf of, creation. When we sing or read them they express and deepen our sense of awe and reverence for the cosmos. As we tend to take more care of what we hold in awe, to foster a reverential attitude to God's creation through psalmody can be one of the greenest things we do. We can now see how the abbot's care that the times for the Work of God be signalled faithfully is more than simply a matter of punctuality; rather, it fits into the overall care fostered by the Rule for all God has made.

So this section of the Rule contains an impressive 'care package', a set of principles around how we should treat our fellow humans and the earth's resources reverently. We need now to look at how the Rule can help us take more care of the highly specific gift God has given each of us: ourselves.

'Let all things be done with moderation' (RB 48:9)

'Take care!' How often do we say this to others? But do we take sufficient care of ourselves? Not in the pampering way that RB 4:12 warns against ('Do not love a soft lifestyle'), nor simply so that we may go on functioning well to serve our families and communities, though this is, of course, important. The ground of our caring for self is that each of us is a unique part of God's creation, made in God's image, a vital member of Christ's body, and thus to be reverenced. As Paul reminded the Corinthians: 'You do not belong to yourself; you have been bought at a price. So glorify God in your body' (1 Cor. 6.19, my translation).

Benedict's prescriptions around care for the individual contain nothing magical: regular, balanced meals, sufficient unbroken sleep, manual labour, much of it outside in his day, providing exercise and fresh air. There is, to use Benedict's own words, 'nothing harsh or burdensome' (Prol. 46) in what is laid down in the Rule, which is further marked by flexibility to individual needs. So the sick may take baths whenever necessary and may eat meat to aid their recovery (RB 36:8–9); the old and children are allowed to anticipate the regular hours for meals (RB 37) and should be given work that occupies but does not overwhelm them (RB 48:24).

However, such are the demands and pressures of life nowadays, especially perhaps on those of middle years who have both the elderly and the young in their care, as well the responsibilities of jobs and homes, that the simplest thing, such as eating regularly, can become complicated. The work–life balance is easily disrupted.

We can't revert to being sixth-century monks – and this applies to twenty-first-century monks and nuns as much as to lay people. But perhaps this Lent we can find guidelines to help pull our lives back into some sort of equilibrium.

Mind the gap!

Chapter 48 of the Rule sets out a typical monastic day: periods of reading/study and work are interwoven with attendance at offices and meals. There is even the possibility of a siesta after lunch. It sounds wonderful! Typical monastic days are not all that common in our monasteries today and perhaps were not as standardized as we might think even in Benedict's day. Then, seasonal adjustments had to be made to make the most of daylight hours, and there were always threats of poor harvests and possible invasion. We tend to underplay these aspects of life in the past and the pressures they must have exerted, and can end up thinking that we moderns have a monopoly on stress!

But the basic structure of a balanced day is there: work, *lectio divina*, rest, meals and prayer are integrated on a daily basis and in one chapter of the Rule. We noted in Chapter 4 that there is no separate chapter on *lectio divina* in the Rule, and here we see that RB 48, 'On the Daily Manual Labour', is about far more than work. So perhaps the first way the Rule can help us with the work–life balance is to question our attitude. Do we think of 'life' and 'work' in opposition, or do we see work, however humble, and including the unpaid work that is the lot of so many, as a necessary part of life? Somehow each person has to find ways to bridge the perceived gap between 'work' and 'life'. Key to this in the Benedictine way, as mentioned in Chapter 5, is learning to stop.

Starting to stop and stopping to start: a closer look at RB 48

Another way of reading this chapter of the Rule is to focus on how often the monks stop what they are doing and move on to the next thing: 'At the first signal, all put away their work to be ready for the second signal' (RB 48:12).

In our monastery, aspirants thinking about a vocation spend three weeks living alongside the nuns. I remember as an aspirant that initially all this stopping and changing tasks every half hour or so was frustrating, but by the end of the three weeks I began to feel the benefit of such a rhythm and found in it a dynamism that energized me. I tried, in a modified way, to carry over this pattern into my busy life as a teacher on returning to 'normal' life, for example by starting the day with some psalms and trying to stop to re-gather myself spiritually in the middle of the day.

It is undoubtedly difficult to stop in today's frenetic culture but our sanity depends on finding ways to do so. Donald Nicholl has written persuasively on this topic,[3] reminding us that the first thing we need to learn about any piece of powerful machinery – including the human body – is how to stop it. He goes on to describe hurry as a form of violence exercised on God's time in order to make it our own.[4] Not only do we not belong to ourselves, we do not own time. By consciously stopping and turning to God at intervals throughout the day, our relationship with time is gradually altered. We learn to receive each moment as a gift to be lived as fully as possible, something the terminally ill, with their heightened sense of the gift of each moment, can often teach us.

In churches of the Eastern tradition, before the start of the Divine Liturgy, the deacon proclaims, 'It is time – *kairos* – for the Lord to act.' The service that follows is therefore seen as the intersection of chronological time (*chronos*) and God's time (*kairos*), the eternity into which those participating are drawn. The same dynamic applies in the West. When we attend or say any part of the office ourselves, we step out of chronological time into God's time, where our inner selves, made for eternity, can breathe more easily. Almost always we return to the day's demands in a better frame of mind.

We may not be able to find space for such structured prayer during the day but, if trying to regain balance is a priority for us, we can find similar breathing spaces opening up as gifts. It all depends on being attentive to these opportunities: the pause at traffic lights, delayed trains or lengthy queues at the supermarket all offer the chance simply 'to be' and to give thanks for life.

When we first start to build in deliberate stops through the day we shall probably have to apply the brakes fairly hard – the bell for an office has this effect in the monastery. But gradually we shall find that time comes to exert less of a tyranny on us. We may notice ourselves slowing down and doing what has to be done at any particular moment more attentively. When we stop rushing we are more fully alive to the present moment. According to the fourteenth-century mystic Meister Eckhart, wisdom consists in doing the next thing you have to do, putting your whole heart into that task and taking delight in it.[5] Benedict would surely applaud such a dictum, and we shall find ourselves less stressed if we try to start stopping. Our Muslim brothers and sisters have much to teach us here through their faithful fivefold punctuation of the day with prayers.

But Benedictine balance is not a question of attaining a perfectly ordered life, which we engineer by placing a few more weights on this or that side of the scales. It is rather about trying to ensure sufficient gaps – however brief – in the busy day's activities to allow us to tune in to the Holy Spirit, who at every instant is there to help us choose the life-giving option:

> Though the Lord may give you the bread of adversity and the water of affliction, yet your Teacher will not hide himself any more . . . And when you turn to the right or when you turn to the left, your ears shall hear a word behind you, saying, 'This is the way; walk in it.'
> (Isa. 30.20–21)

This gift of discretion, taught by the Holy Spirit, was something St Gregory the Great singled out as a remarkable feature of Benedict's Rule.[6] It helps to make us supple in response to changing circumstances; it teaches us, for example, whether to press on with a difficult task or to give in and have a hot bath and an early night. That same Holy Spirit who hovered over the waters at the start, bringing light out of darkness and order out of chaos (Gen. 1.2), will do the same in our life, helping us to prioritize and ordering our days from within.

Above all, the Holy Spirit will remind us, when we do stop to tune in, not only what to do but, even more importantly, that God is always with us as we journey through Lent and life. 'When he calls on me, I will answer', runs the Lenten psalm (Ps. 91/90.15).

At base, like so much on the Benedictine way, balance, which is part of reverence for self, is the outcome of listening, that golden thread running through the Rule that we considered in Chapters 1, 3 and 4.

'On Sunday all are to be engaged in reading' (RB 48:22)

God rested on the Sabbath day after all the work of creation (see Gen. 2.2). Of course he did not need to and, as Jesus points out in the gospel, his Father goes on working even on the Sabbath: giving life, healing, judging the dead and sustaining the whole universe in being (John 5.17). This day of rest, Sunday for Christians, is given for our benefit as an opportunity to refresh body, mind and spirit, and also as a symbol of the eternal rest in God's presence towards which we journey on earth. The Letter to the Hebrews alludes to this, still using the word 'sabbath', which has carried over in our day beyond Jewish circles: 'A Sabbath rest still remains for the people of God ... Let us therefore make every effort to enter that rest' (Heb. 4.9, 11).

We saw in Chapter 5 the centrality of Sunday, the day of the Lord's resurrection, in the way Benedict has structured the running of the monastery. Here in RB 48 the implication is that work on Sunday is kept to what is necessary, so that the monks may be free to listen to the Word speaking to their hearts, both in church and in their personal reading, and to rest in prayer.[7]

The degradation of Sunday into another working day is a huge topic with far-reaching cultural causes and ramifications beyond the scope of a short Lent book, but we are all aware of the shift and, I think, mostly lament it. Current cultural norms pose a significant challenge to Christians who would practise their faith, but the positive thing is that we can do something about it. This time it is to our Jewish brothers and sisters that we can look for inspiration from their faithful keeping of Shabbat.

Needless to say, there is always work to be done on a Sunday. Benedict recognizes that those with various duties will not be as free to read as the others. But from his determination that help shall be given to anyone facing heavy work in the monastery, be it the cellarer (RB 31:17–19), the porter (RB 66:5), the guest kitchen cooks (RB 53:18), or anyone else under pressure (RB 53:19–20), we can be fairly confident that the necessary Sunday jobs of cooking, caring for the sick and guests or tending livestock would have been shared. Again it is a question of attitude. While some Christians may, for economic reasons, find themselves in a position where they are obliged to work on a Sunday, for many there is a real choice about, say, whether to shop on a Sunday, whether to do chores that can be done on a Saturday, whether and how much to use the internet.

In a pressured week, Sundays well kept can offer time not only to read and pray but to commune with family, friends and nature and to reach out to those who are alone and would value some company. Once we accept that trying to keep Sunday special is worthwhile, we can be creative in finding ways to do that which fit our circumstances.

On the observance of Lent: RB 49

Looking forward with the joy of spiritual desire to the holy feast of Easter.
(RB 49:7)

When it comes to instructions about Lent, Benedict departs radically from his template, the Rule of the Master. The latter devotes about six pages to Lent in a 'Rule for Lent' within the wider Rule. In contrast, Benedict offers just over half a page on the season. For him, as we have seen, the life of a monk should be a continuous Lent, a constant looking forward to Easter; a life devoted to prayer, the Scriptures and self-restraint. So as we have been suggesting throughout, the whole Rule is, in a sense, a Lent book.

A Benedictine Lent is not a heroic feat of ascetical endurance but more an attempt to live the life to which one is committed more faithfully. Or, as Benedict puts it, 'to wash away the negligences of other times' (RB 49:3).

Perhaps in RB 49 we can see Benedict pointing the monks back to RB 48, to the balance sketched there between work and prayer, reading and rest. Certainly, there is some comfort in thinking that the monks slipped into carelessness and neglect of their spiritual lives, as we do, and that Lent was seen as a re-adjusting, via deeper attention to silence, prayer and *lectio*, of areas that had become unbalanced.

But the encouraging thing is that the chapter is not written so much in a mode of pulling up one's socks as of rekindling one's desire for Easter, not surely simply the Easter that will come at the end of the 40 days of Lent but the eternal life with God that is the gift of Easter and the monk's deepest quest.

> In these days [of Lent] . . . let each one offer God something of his own free will, over and above the usual measure of service and in the joy of the Holy Spirit.
> (RB 49:5–6)

Benedict is not directive when it comes to guidelines on the observance of Lent. There is a considerable freedom afforded the monks in choosing what they wish to give up or take on, which shows trust in their level of self-knowledge – though they must let the abbot know what they plan. He would probably veto any attempts at the sort of standing all night in freezing rivers beloved of the fervent Celtic monks.

So there are helpful things we can take away from Benedict's short chapter on Lent: first of all, to keep the Easter focus uppermost and to do all in the Holy Spirit, which is already Christ's Easter gift to us; then, to see it as a 'holy season', which helps foster our 'wholeness' and prepares us to be drawn more fully into Christ's resurrected life at Easter; to recall that small adjustments are probably more effective than highly ambitious ones; to be open to the idea that there is probably something quite personal that God is asking of us this Lent that we need to discern in prayer.

Perhaps we can think of a Lent partner who might take the place of the abbot in holding us to our intention and advising us if it seems too harsh.

Some blessings of reverence

Given the eco-crisis in which we live, it is perhaps not over-dramatic to name the survival of the planet as probably the greatest blessing that we can hope for through our reverent attitude to the earth. 'Blessed are the gentle for they shall inherit the earth' (Matt. 5.5, my translation).

We need not rehearse here the negative scenarios around climate change and the degradation of the earth as a sustainable place for life. And while large-scale initiatives like the Paris Climate Agreement are vital, just as important are the small steps we can each take, ranging from reducing our consumption of petrol/diesel, to car sharing, recycling and keeping wonder at the beauty of the earth alive in our singing of the psalms. After all, 'care' and 'cure' have a common root in the Latin *curare*, which we saw features prominently in this section of the Rule.

Pope Francis's ground-breaking publication on the environment, *Laudato Si': On Care for Our Common Home* (2015), is notable for the way it includes human beings and their flourishing as part of the environmental challenge.

With its reverence for human beings and the earth's resources, the Rule of Benedict anticipated many of our ecological concerns and can still provide a 'green-print' to help us think globally and act locally.

For reflection and action

1 Think about how you might build more 'stops' into your day.
2 (a) Spend some definite time – a day, half a day or an hour, or whatever suits you – in noticing *how* you do things.

(b) On another day, spend the same amount of time trying to do things more attentively.

(c) You may find it helpful to share your findings with a friend or in a small group.

3 Either personally or as a parish, think about a green audit during Lent, with an action plan to follow up through the year.

7

The blessing of welcoming: RB 53–72

Let all guests who present themselves be welcomed as Christ.
(RB 53:1)

If Benedictines are known for anything it is for their hospitality. The last third of Benedict's Rule opens out to welcome the stranger, the poor, pilgrims, visiting monks and would-be candidates for monastic life. But these chapters are also concerned with hospitality in the broader sense and provide guidelines for welcoming one another, the unexpected and even the impossible. All Christians are called to go out to others in a lifelong 'exodus' to the promised land of eternal life. Each Lent we recapitulate this journey away from self towards the other, and in this chapter we shall explore how the Rule can assist that migration.

Benedictine hospitality in context

That humans can be hospitable is surely one of the more heart-warming features of humanity. Yet 'hospitality' resonates with words like 'hostility' and 'hostage'. This ambivalence can be found in the Latin: *hospes* means 'host', 'guest' or 'stranger', and echoes *hostis*, meaning 'stranger' or even 'enemy'. Here, language developments seem to condense a triumph of positive forces over harmful ones; sympathy for the vulnerability of the stranger winning out over fear and mistrust so that the potential enemy becomes a guest.

Such a shift away from the closed-ness of the tribe is encoded in our genetic make-up, for despite the efforts of some to engineer a 'pure' race, we are mostly, and blessedly, mongrels. Today, more than ever, we need to cultivate a trusting welcome towards those who appear different but who share our common humanity. Sometimes the cost will be high. Remember the steadfast trust of the Trappist monk Christian de Chergé and his brethren of Tibhirine, Algeria. Refusing to leave their adopted country in the face of growing hostility and the almost certain fate that awaited them, they became martyrs of Christian–Muslim dialogue in May 1996.[1]

Then, before it is a monastic virtue, to welcome is a Judaeo-Christian one, rooted in the culture of the Middle East with the patriarchs, Abraham and Sarah as icons of hospitality (Gen. 18). The New Testament continues this tradition where both the setting for, and content of, Jesus' teaching is often one of table hospitality (see Mark 2.15–17; Luke 7.36–50). The parable of the Sheep and the Goats (Matt. 25.31–46) makes it clear that we shall be judged on whether we have welcomed others as Christ.

For the desert monks and nuns this gospel precept of hospitality was central. They would keep back part of their meagre allotment of food each day, recounts Cassian, in order to 'refresh Christ' in any guest who happened to visit, and could even break their fast for the sake of hospitality.[2]

From this stream of human, biblical and monastic tradition flows Benedict's teaching on hospitality, where all guests are to be received as Christ (RB 53:1), the superior may break the fast for the sake of a guest (RB 53:10), and all are treated with humanity, regardless of rank. And where, further, special care is to be shown for the poor (RB 53:15) – a precept Benedict has added to the Master's text he was editing.

So Benedictine hospitality grows out of the spiritual teaching of the Bible and especially the gospel. As such, it has a claim on all Christians, not simply those who live in monasteries.

'As we progress in this way of life and in faith, our hearts will expand . . .' (RB Prol. 49)

'This way of life . . .'[3]

If we remember back to the start of the Rule, where Benedict sets out its goal (that is, to lead us to eternal life through following the gospel precepts), he promises that those who are faithful to the way he is charting will experience an expansion of heart. In other words, they will grow in their capacity to love through the Holy Spirit 'poured into our hearts' (see Rom. 5.5).

Chapter 4 of the Rule, the 'Tools of Good Works', sketched out in some detail the demands and character of this Christian love that embraces even the enemy and does good to the stranger and needy. As its title suggests, that chapter also provided some of the tools necessary for us to cultivate such an open-hearted love that is beyond our fallen human nature: 'to listen readily to holy readings and to pray frequently' (RB 4:55–56). In Chapters 3 and 4 of this book we looked in more detail at how much of the Rule is taken up with nurturing the inner life of prayer and the role of the Bible, both heard in the liturgy and pondered personally, in purifying the heart.

So we see that the whole thrust of the Rule is about welcoming: opening our hearts to welcome Christ the Word; opening ourselves in prayer to welcome the Trinity and, from these encounters, welcoming and serving our neighbour in a spirit of reverence that extends also to the environment and material creation.

Far from being an 'add on', then, this section of the Rule, on hospitality (RB 53–72), can be seen as a natural, or rather supernatural, conclusion to all that has gone before, from the Prologue to RB 52. Faithfulness to prayer, to *lectio divina* and to the challenges of community, family and parish life, will expand our hearts and enable us to try to welcome those – however different from us – who cross our paths in life.

'In faith . . .'

For the Rule to become a life-giving guide it must be read with the eyes of faith and acted on in faith. One is free to accept or reject the invitation of the Prologue to take the Rule as a guide, but it will only bring life if we see Christ in the guest (RB 53:1, 7, 15), in the sick (RB 36:1), the superior (RB 2:2) and in one another (RB 71). Such a view is nothing less than the gospel demands: 'in so far as you did this to one of the least of these brothers of mine, you did it to me' (Matt. 25.40, NJB). While faith is a gift of our baptism, it does require constant vigilance and nurturing through Scripture, the sacraments and personal prayer. There is a discipline involved, an *ascesis* or training, which retrains our initial reactions to people and events and helps us act in accordance with our deepest beliefs, 'in faith'. It is no coincidence that we use the verb 'to practise' when it comes to hospitality! We know in our hearts that every person is a child of God created in his image, but sometimes people present themselves with this image heavily disguised, just as we ourselves do to others.

Chapter 53 of the Rule, with its elaborate ritual for welcoming guests, can, with some twenty-first-century adaptations, help us. We greet warmly, we smile, we take an interest, we show reverence, we lead to prayer, we allow space. And very often faith works miracles of transformation as Christ in the guest emerges to meet Christ in us.

Benedict seems to be well aware of the need for this form of asceticism – far more demanding than giving up sugar for Lent – as he calls the chapter on welcoming candidates to the monastic life 'The *Discipline* of Receiving Brothers' (RB 58).

The same dynamic of acting in faith, trying to do the right thing, giving people their due even when they seem to be distant or acting unpredictably, can be applied in all relationships in any community or family setting.

Welcoming as receiving

If the above sounds rather hard work, a closer look at this part of the Rule may provide some encouragement. In the last chapter we found the idea of 'care' running through the core of the Rule. I'd like to suggest that what colours RB 53–72 is the concept of 'receiving'. Words of the *suscipere* family ('to receive' is one of its meanings in Latin) occur 28 times across the whole Rule, 25 of those occurrences concentrated in the section we are looking at. Here are some examples:

On the Reception [*Suscipiendis*] of Guests.
(title RB 53)

The greatest care should be shown in the receiving [*susceptioni*] of the poor and pilgrims because in them especially Christ is received [*suscipitur*].
(RB 53:15)

If the novice promises to obey . . . let him be received [*suscipiatur*] into the community.
(RB 58:14)

Three of the references to 'receive' occur, unsurprisingly, in RB 54, 'On Whether Monks Should Receive [*Suscipere*] Letters' or gifts. But this is the key! Monks and nuns have nothing of their own. The liberating flipside is that they receive everything, including relationships, as gifts. That fundamental truth applies to every human being no matter how rich: there are no pockets in a shroud. If we allow this deep truth to permeate our hearts, everything changes: the guest, no matter how unexpected, the difficult neighbour or colleague, can become a gift to be received.

'If a brother be commanded impossible tasks' (RB 68)

We see this transforming power of the gift mindset in RB 68, one of Benedict's miniature masterpieces worth quoting in full:

If something difficult or impossible be enjoined upon any brother, let him receive the superior's command with all gentleness and obedience. But if he should see that the weight of the burden completely exceeds the measure of his strength, let him patiently, and at the right moment,

explain to his superior why such is impossible. This should be done without pride, obstinacy or contradiction. If after [the monk's] representations, the superior's command remains unchanged, then the junior must recognize that it is to his advantage, and let him obey out of love, trusting in the help of God.
(RB 68)

I can confirm that this chapter works. Once, having proclaimed that I would do any job in the monastery except look after the bees, imagine my reaction at being landed with that very job! In desperation I reached for RB 68. It comes down to trying to make 'yes' our default answer, of cultivating an openness and a willingness to override initial negativity – with discretion, of course: I would not have jumped off the church tower. I ended up loving the bees and was very sorry when we had to give them up. A whole new world had opened up, a gift I would have missed had I refused outright what had seemed an 'impossible' ask.

Receiving as listening

The most challenging gifts to receive are often those nearest and dearest to us in our families and communities. We may make an effort for guests but the demands of the home team are, well, more demanding. They see us in all our moods and brokenness and limitations. But we know that this is where we are called to grow both personally and into a deeper communion with them and through them with God, and that our deepest joys are also to be found here. Benedict's chapter 71, 'On Mutual Obedience', puts it like this:

> Obedience is a blessing to be shown by all not only to the
> abbot but the brothers should likewise show obedience
> to each other knowing that it is by this way of obedience
> that they go to God.
> (RB 71:1–2)

We may think we've strayed into a different section of the Rule
with the mention of obedience here but we are still very much
in the realm of 'receiving'. When you come to think of it, what
are we doing when we receive someone but opening our hearts
and listening to that person?

We listen at several levels: to how those around us seem on
the surface, how perhaps their body language is saying something different. But at depth we try to listen in faith to their
deepest truth: we believe this person to be a child of God.
Here we find mutuality even when more superficial behaviour or attitudes may be quite contrary. Each step on the path
of receiving one another at this deepest level draws us more
profoundly into the completely frictionless communion of the
Trinity. We gradually learn to see others as God sees them,
in that 'divinizing light' (*deificum lumen*) of the Prologue
(Prol. 9), and in the process, the image of God in ourselves is
gradually purified; we become divinized.

Sometimes, though, it takes a courageous step down to
advance on this way. The desire for peace and reconciliation
and a willingness to give way to the other beyond the need to
establish who was right is beautifully portrayed at the end of
RB 71:

> If [a brother] get the impression that any senior is dis-
> pleased or angry with him, however slightly, let him at

once, without delay, prostrate at his feet and lie there until
the disturbance is healed by a blessing.
(RB 71:7–8)

Rather than being an invitation to be a doormat, this precept
actually invites the junior to Christlikeness. Prostrations in the
living room or office are probably a bit over the top, but sometimes a cup of tea, a smile or just a silent, but not sullen refusal
to go down the road of arguing can be effective first moves,
'pre-emptive strikes' that maintain or restore peace.

Deo gratias: Thanks be to God! RB 66:3

Most commentators see RB 66 as a primitive end of the Rule.
It includes a vivid description of the porter of the monastery,
someone who seems to sum up in himself Benedictine hospitality and much of the Rule:

> At the door of the monastery let there be placed a wise
> old man who knows how to give and take a message and
> whose age will prevent him from wandering about . . .
> As soon as anyone knocks, or a poor man cries out, let
> [the porter] answer, 'Thanks be to God' or 'Your blessing,
> please'. Then let him attend to them promptly with all the
> gentleness of the fear of God and the warmth of love.
> (RB 66:1, 3–4)

In the novitiate we were taught to reply *Deo gratias* ('Thanks be
to God') when anyone knocked on the door of our cell. At first
I thought it was a quaint monastic custom but in time came
to see this in the light of the porter's response above. It spoke
to me of someone who, after many years in the monastery,

had learned to welcome the unpredictable demand as gift, something for which to give thanks. I'm afraid this rather contrasted with my own inner reaction as a novice to any knock on the door, which was to see it as an interruption of whatever I was doing. But since working in the guest department myself for quite a long time, I hope I may have grown nearer to the porter's approach. To be drawn out of oneself towards others is always a blessing, something for which to thank God.

Blessings of welcoming

One of the main blessings of welcoming is that through it we receive new life, both quantitatively via the reception of new members, be they candidates, oblates, friends or associates, and qualitatively through the gifts and talents that newcomers bring to the community, parish or our family and friendship networks. Practising hospitality demands energy but is also revitalizing: there is nothing like working in guest ministry if you are feeling a bit down. Guests are – almost always – appreciative of the blessings of the monastery: the silence, the services, the beauty of the church and the grounds, and are generous in the way they feed this back to the community.

There seems to be one of those gospel reversals around hospitality: it really is in giving that one receives. The Rule reflects this, for after the monks have welcomed a guest – Christ – the community recites: 'O God, we have received your mercy in the midst of your temple' (RB 53:14; see Ps. 48/47.10). Fast-forward to the Emmaus gospel (Luke 24.13ff.), and we can almost hear these words on the lips of Cleopas and his companion as it dawns on them that the stranger they welcomed and who took the role of host at their own table was the risen Christ himself.

There is another reversal in the vow ceremony (RB 58:21). Having placed the chart of profession on the altar, the novice intones: 'Receive [another *suscipe*] me, Lord, according to your word and I shall live. Let not my hope in you be disappointed' (see Ps 119/118.116). Oblates do the same after making their promise or oblation. In both cases, the prayer is one of asking to be welcomed by God and upheld by him on the journey through life. Poignantly, this prayer is repeated at monastic funerals when, God willing, the deceased will be welcomed into the tents of eternity.

An implication of this prayer to be received by God is that we – monks, nuns, oblates, seekers – are all guests in God's house. Where this realization has been truly assimilated by the community, visitors, even strangers, feel at home in their Father's house. This is a blessing to cultivate in our day when so many people experience a sense of rootlessness.

Welcoming fosters resilience

Since the 1970s the concept of 'resilience' has been gaining ground in the field of psychology as a useful way to speak of a person's ability to bounce back from negative situations. Originally borrowed from physics, where it refers to the capacity of materials to resist shock or stress, the human reality of resilience goes rather further in that people can grow through adversity rather than simply recoil to a previously held position or state.

'Acceptance of the other as a person . . . is often regarded as a foundation stone of resilience.'[4] I am convinced that the culture of welcoming acceptance promoted by the Rule is foundational to Benedictine stability (one of the Benedictine vows[5]). Further, the asceticism of trying to welcome and accept things that run counter to our will trains us in resilience so that when the unexpected hits us, whether it be the dreaded redundancy letter, the unwelcome medical test results or anything else, we are more likely to be enabled to stand firm and grow through the experience.

As with many spiritual phenomena, things work also the other way. Benedictine stability – sticking things out here rather than fleeing to perceived greener pastures there – helps to foster welcoming acceptance because when we are pushed to the limit, we are more likely to cry out with urgent, heartfelt prayer to God for help. And he always hears us.

You may recall that at the end of the 'Tools of Good Works', the workshops where the monk is to make use of all these spiritual tools are 'the cloisters of the monastery and stability in the community' (RB 4:78). For a monk, nun or oblate this means that one makes one's commitment to the community of people living in the monastery more than to the monastic building. So to move the location of a monastery, as my own community did in 2009, is not to breach the commitment of stability that exists among the members of the monastic community. Families who move house are still united to one another; parish communities who face the closure of their church building retain their living bonds of charity with one another. The ongoing challenge for all is to practise hospitality towards one another where one lives.

In RB 72, the last full chapter of the Rule if we take RB 73 as a kind of appendix, we see the great blessing that 'welcoming', in its broadest sense, can bring about. Again, it is worth quoting the whole chapter:

Just as there is an evil zeal of bitterness which separates from God and leads to hell, so there is a good zeal which separates from vices and leads to God and eternal life. Let monks foster this zeal with all the fervour of love. Let them, that is, give way to one another in honour. Let them bear with the greatest patience one another's weaknesses both of body and behaviour. Let them compete in showing obedience to one another. Let no one follow what seems good for themselves but rather what is good for the other. Let them practise fraternal charity with pure love. Let them show loving reverend dread for God, and sincere, humble love for their abbot. Let them prefer nothing whatsoever to Christ. And may he bring us all together to eternal life.

(RB 72)

Benedict concludes his Rule with a portrait of a community – 'warts and all' – united in mutual love and reverence as they follow Christ who is the focus of the single-hearted love of each of them. The 'weaknesses of body and behaviour' have not been airbrushed out. They are being carried 'in Christ' by the Christ-self in every member of the community. The resurrection of Christ which Easter proclaims, central to the Rule, and towards which we journey in Lent, is the greatest act of resilience ever enacted. Through the resurrection, Jesus not only rebounded from the most appallingly adverse situation of affliction and death but has, ever since, been drawing disciples after him to an eternal life that starts now.

Thanks be to God – *Deo gratias*!

For reflection and action

1 Read RB 53 and RB 72 prayerfully.
2 Read Romans 12 prayerfully.

3 Do you notice any similarities between Paul's exhortation to the Romans and Benedict's to his monks?

4 Is there anything in RB 72 that you think might help you on your Christian journey after Easter?

8

Epilogue: The blessing of 'beyond'

The full observance of justice is not laid down in this Rule.
(RB 73: title)

It is perhaps even more challenging to conclude a piece of writing than to begin. How do you end a guide to life that is still unfolding?

Benedict manages something of a coup at the conclusion of his Rule, giving us, in the twenty or so lines of RB 73, an ending that opens out rather than closes down, an epilogue that is really a 'non-ending' that invites us into the 'beyond'.

It occurs to me that this is what has been going on throughout the Rule, of which the goal from the outset has been 'eternal life' (see Prol. 17). Theologians would describe this pull of the 'beyond' as an eschatological focus. So as we consider RB 73 at the end of our Lenten journey, we shall also look back briefly at some of the themes already considered and, I hope, catch some shafts of this light of eternity shining through the Rule.

The title of the last chapter of the Rule is rather odd: 'The Full Observance of Justice Is Not Laid Down in This Rule'. This would probably not pass muster with many publishers today. It is the complete opposite of all those positive things we read on the back of books encouraging us to buy them! But as it points beyond itself, this title incarnates the Benedictine humility that the Rule teaches.

Similarly, the advice for 'further reading' that Benedict includes in this chapter cannot be what it seems initially. He recommends we read the Old and New Testaments as well as the early Christian and monastic fathers. But these have been the staple reading/listening of the monks throughout the Rule. This is surely also an invitation to deepen our reading of these primary, life-giving sources, which Benedict presents as true guides for life and as aids to help us journey towards our Creator (see RB 73:3–5). Here lies the burden of the final chapter: to impel readers forward on the spiritual journey to God.

Hastening towards our heavenly homeland (see RB 73:2, 8)

As Paul reminded the Philippians, 'Our citizenship is in heaven' (Phil. 3.20). God's people, ever since Abraham (Gen. 12), have been nomads on a journey to occupy no earthly territory but that 'better country' (Heb. 11.16) where they will be at home with God for ever. Remember that the opening paragraph of the Rule calls us back to God and sets us off on that return journey (Prol. 2). Jesus, by his death, resurrection and ascension, has opened the way back for us. Without such a dynamic pull heavenwards, any Christian community – any Christian – can become discouraged by current difficulties and lacking in energy.

We need hope for the long haul, the hope that comes from looking forward to something and that strengthens us in present trials. And it is just this vista that opens up throughout the Rule, elevating every least activity in the monastery.

RB 4:46 urges us 'to long for eternal life with all spiritual desire', while the following admonition to 'keep death daily before [our] eyes' (RB 4:47) surely also embraces this promise of our heavenly homeland, as well as a more sober call to amend one's behaviour. And 'never to lose hope in God's mercy' is the final 'tool' for gospel living with which we are provided in RB 4:74.

At the end of that same chapter you may recall that Benedict, rather than going into detail, draws on Paul's words to the Corinthians to hint at the delights we can hope for in the next world: 'What no eye has seen, nor ear heard, nor the human heart conceived, what God has prepared for those who love him' (1 Cor. 2.9). Still, it can be a help to have some idea of what heaven might be for us: God gives us good desires so that he can fulfil and surpass them. For me, heaven would include the sea, Monteverdi's *Vespers*, being reunited with loved ones and no more winters, as well, of course, as the hope of seeing 'my Pilot face to face/ When I have crost the bar'.[1]

You may like to draw up your own list.

Meanwhile, there are blessings in being still pilgrims on the earth (see Ps. 39/38.13). Solomon reputedly had a ring made inscribed with the words 'This too will pass'. There is a certain peace that comes from knowing that negative situations of any kind have a limit. But Christian hope in the resurrection gives us a more positive, deeper, joyful peace of the risen Christ. Peace in a crown of thorns is the Benedictine motto, and it comes to us from 'beyond'.

'Seek first the kingdom of God' (Matt. 6.33; RB 2:35)

The otherworldliness that should characterize the lives of all Christians does not imply a flight from the world but rather a radical way of living in, and engaging with, that world which God made and loves. An early Christian text, probably written to explain Christianity to pagans in the Roman Empire in the middle of the second century, puts it like this:

> The difference between Christians and the rest of humanity is not one of nationality, or language or customs . . . They pass their lives in whatever place each one's lot has determined . . . Nevertheless, their communities show some features which are unusual . . . Although they are residents at home in their own nations, their behaviour is more like people who are 'resident aliens' . . . For them, any country is a fatherland and any fatherland a foreign country . . . Though providence has placed them here in the flesh, they do not live according to the flesh; their days are passed on earth but their citizenship is in heaven . . . They show love to all and are persecuted by all. They are misunderstood and condemned but by suffering death they are quickened into life . . . In short, the relation of Christians to the world is like that of the soul to the body: as the soul is diffused through every part of the body, so are Christians spread through all the cities of the world.[2]

Even though Benedict's monks did live apart from 'the world' physically, then as now there was much necessary commerce with the world outside the monastery, and then as now a danger that negative aspects – all that the First Letter of John would term 'the world' – might infiltrate the cloister. We can apply this to the Christian home. The abbot is exhorted to 'Seek first the kingdom of God' (RB 2:35) – a gospel precept (Matt. 6.33). The Rule helps those who follow it to prioritize kingdom values in everyday life and to try to discern the will of God in any situation. This will often lead to counter-cultural decisions that put long-term benefits, say to the environment, before short-term financial gains. On the domestic front, it may mean prioritizing involvement of the elderly or frail in tasks that could be done more 'efficiently' by someone younger and fitter. Here reverence for the person is the kingdom value being sought.

But essentially the kingdom of God is an interior reality, and it is through the spiritual growth of each individual Christian, by God's grace, that the kingdom breaks into the world.

'What is not possible to us by nature, let us ask the Lord to supply by the aid of his grace' (Prol. 41)

We saw how this call to live beyond fallen human nature into the fullness of our God-given nature, announced to the monk at the beginning of the Rule, is at the heart of the Christian vocation. The Rule is a practical document designed to help us fulfil this vocation but it will only help us on the spiritual path if we put it into practice. Benedict says as much in the opening lines of RB 73: 'We have drafted this Rule so that by practising it in monasteries we may show ourselves to have some integrity in our behaviour and to have made a start at monastic life' (RB 73:1). Remember that in the Prologue Benedict wanted to set down 'nothing harsh or burdensome' (Prol. 46) but also warned us not to be daunted by the narrowness of the path to that fullness of life promised in the gospel (Prol. 48).

Another key precept that Benedict lays down for the abbot, and that is useful for anyone in a leadership position, is that everything should be arranged 'so that the strong have something to yearn for and the weak nothing to run from' (RB 64:19). All are called to go beyond themselves – to grow spiritually – but in a gentle way, adapted to individual capacities. Benedict's language in this concluding chapter, 'let's show we've made a start at monastic life' and 'keep this little Rule for beginners' (RB 73:1, 8), shows him to be an abbot who practises what he preaches. He has imbued his Rule with that same mix of encouragement to mature into our full potential as human beings made in the image and likeness of God, combined with tender understanding for our human frailty, whether it be shown in oversleeping and being late for prayer (RB 11:11–13) or more serious lapses in charity (RB 70).

Such tenderness towards human frailty does not mean that 'anything goes', however. The way of Benedict is demanding – how can it not be when it is a guide to living the uncompromising challenges of the gospel? We saw above that the call to gospel living enshrined in RB 4 is based on the Beatitudes. To see the persecuted, poor and hungry as 'blessed' makes sense only in the context of the kingdom of God inaugurated by Jesus Christ, which is so contrary to the ways of the world. It is impossible for fallen human nature to live up to the standards Jesus set in the Sermon on the Mount, around love of enemies, forgiveness and non-retaliation, but to these standards we are called. Baptism equips us with necessary gifts of grace, at least in embryo.

In Chapters 3 and 4 of this book we explored how exposure to God in prayer and the Word of God can expand our hearts to receive this grace, the light of the Holy Spirit. Growth in the Spirit in turn affects our spiritual senses: we begin to grow in attentiveness, to listen with the ears of the heart beyond surface meanings; we begin to see with the eyes of faith, beyond appearances. And as part of the discipline of the Benedictine way, we attempt to practise all these things even when we don't necessarily feel them. We *believe* that Christ is present in the abbot, the sick, the guest, the stranger, showing reverence for all people and all of creation (Chapters 6 and 7). Through the power of Word and Spirit, the Rule is transformative, not simply pointing us towards what is beyond – the transcendent – but facilitating the transformation of the lives of those who follow it.

In short, the Rule beckons and aids us, by its structured practices, to live according to God's immense vision for us – we could call it a vision of wholeness or holiness – to live with his life, to be transfigured by the 'deifying light' (Prol. 9). A possible translation of the title of RB 73 is 'That this Rule is only the Beginning of Holiness'.[3]

To grow in this path we do not need to change our state of life or enter a monastery. Down the centuries, and increasingly over the past 50 years, those living in the world have found the Rule a sure guide to living out the sort of integrity between faith professed and life lived that marks the witness of the earliest Christians. Probably what makes the Rule such a powerful document is that, while grounding those who follow it in the immediacy of everyday life, it keeps their gaze fixed on the values of God's kingdom both as it will be at the end of time and as it breaks in to transform life now.

'And from heaven we expect a Saviour, our Lord Jesus Christ' (Phil. 3.20, my translation)

Throughout this book we have reflected on Benedict's words that the life of a monk should be a continuous Lent (RB 49:1). One aspect of this is that just as Lent is marked by a longing for Easter, so the whole of a monastic life is marked by a longing for Christ's second coming. The monk or committed Christian is one who keeps vigil for this event in obedience to Jesus' command that we 'stay awake' (Mark 13.37). The long monastic services of Vigils, especially at night or in the early morning, are the liturgical expression of this longing. Whatever else is done in a monastery, the monk or nun and all disciples of Christ are always waiting in hope, living a lifelong Lent orientated towards the 'beyond' from where Christ will come at the end of time. And even now he comes in those strong moments when time and eternity meet in the celebration of the Divine Office (considered in Chapter 5), the Eucharist and other sacraments, as well as in our personal encounters with the transcendent in prayer, the beauty of nature, art, music or deep human relationships. All such moments are blessings of the beyond which strengthen and help us to give witness to others of our God who is great but looks on the lowly (see Mary's song, Luke 1.46–55).

Commentators on the Rule have noticed a similarity in language and style between RB 73 and the Prologue,[4] both apparently written by Benedict himself rather than edited from the Rule of the Master. The details need not detain us but what is important is the significance of this confluence between the end and the beginning of the Rule for our spiritual lives. One thing it suggests is that holiness, the 'end' of the Rule in both senses, is not to be attained by looking for extraordinary spiritual experiences or in exotic locations. Rather, the Rule invites us to holiness by going back to the beginning. We are to start again where we are, to be always beginners, always setting out. Benedict gives us a lifelong programme for Easter and beyond.

Epilogue: The blessing of 'beyond'

I would like to let St Benedict have the last word. In the final lines of the Rule, for the first time since the beginning of the Prologue, he addresses the reader in the singular. It is as if Benedict were looking down the ages to the vast throng who would be helped on their spiritual journey, not only through Lent to Easter but also through this life to the eternal Easter of never-ending light. To each one of us he says, quite personally, with full confidence in God, that by keeping 'this little Rule', with Christ's help, 'you will arrive. Amen'.

Reflection

Oh seek – while the hills remain.
God calls, though daylight fails,
the cruel, the pitiful, the proud,
the weak, the brave, the covetous,
the faltering, the wise, the poor,
the kings, the lepers, and the crowd.
Struck through with death, we hold the seed;
life springs, though our pale roots are dry;
though heaven never seemed so high,
God stoops to touch our need.
And all the ages fall away;
eyes meet, and shoulders touch at last;
Christ waits, and gathers in His day
the present, the future and the past.

(Jane Tyson Clement, 1917–2000)[5]

Notes

1 The blessing of beginning

1 Translations from the Rule of St Benedict are my own. I have used as a base text the translation of Dom Justin McCann OSB, published by the Stanbrook Abbey Press in 1937.

2 Gregory the Great, *Moralia*, Dedicatory Letter, iv. For an English version, see: <www.lectionarycentral.com/gregorymoraliaindex.html>.

3 See Chapter 3, pp. 32–4, 40.

4 The Hebrew enumeration of the Psalms, usually one ahead of the Septuagint, is given first, here and throughout.

2 The blessing of gospel living

1 St Basil, *Short Rules*, 225.

2 Julian of Norwich, *Revelations of Divine Love*, Ch. 68.

3 Opening of the *Didache* (my translation). English versions of this and many of the ancient texts cited may be found online: <www.newadvent.org/fathers/>.

4 G. Collins, *Meeting Christ in His Mysteries*, Columba, Dublin, 2010, pp. 284–97.

5 See also RB 4:47: 'to keep death daily before [our] eyes'; v. 57, 'to confess . . . sins daily'; and v. 63, 'to live by God's commandments every day'.

6 *Crossing Barriers*, Churches Together in Britain and Ireland, London, 2017.

3 The blessing of attentiveness: RB 5–7

1 Augustine Baker OSB, 'The Life of Dame Gertrude More', Ampleforth Abbey MS 125, p. 393. The same manuscript describes 'multiplicitie and distraction' as impediments to contemplative prayer (p. 467).

2 A Carthusian, *The Freedom of Obedience*, Darton, Longman & Todd, London, 1993; A Carthusian, *They Speak by Silence*, Darton, Longman & Todd, London, 1998; M. Casey, *Truthful Living: St Benedict's Teaching on Humility*, Gracewing, Leominster, 2001.

3 S. Weil, *Waiting on God*, Fontana, London, 1959, pp. 66–7.

4 John Cassian mentions 5,000 monks under one abba in the Thebaid in Egypt, *Institutes*, Bk IV, 1.

5 See J. Wortley (tr.), *The Book of the Elders: Sayings of the Desert Fathers, The Systematic Collection*, Liturgical Press, Collegeville, MN, 2012.

6 St Athanasius, *Life of Antony*, 91.

7 For a helpful contemporary guide to Evagrius' teaching, see A. Tilby, *The Seven Deadly Sins*, SPCK, London, 2009.

8 For example, *The Confessions*: 'You have made us for yourself, O God, and our hearts are restless until they rest in you' (Bk 1, 1).

9 Wortley, *The Book of the Elders*, No. 23, p. 379.

10 'The Substance of the Rule of St Bennet', Downside MS 26595, p. 34.

11 Irenaeus, *Against Heresies*, Bk IV, 20, 7.

12 John Henry Newman, *Parochial and Plain Sermons*, Vol. III, Sermon IX.

4 The blessing of the Word

1 K. Fitzherbert, *True to Both My Selves*, Virago, London, 1997, pp. 140–1.

2 St John Chrysostom, *In Gen.* 3, 8: *PG* 53, 134.

3 Irenaeus, *Against Heresies*, Bk V, 21, 14–16.

4 St Augustine, *The Enarrations on the Psalms*, 103, 4, 1: *PL* 37, 1378.

5 St Augustine, *Quaest. in Hept.* 2, 73: *PL* 34, 623.

6 After the ground-breaking synod on the Word of God at Rome in 2008, attended by Christians across the ecumenical spectrum and addressed for the first time ever by a Chief Rabbi, Shear Yashuv Cohen of Haifa, Pope Benedict XVI called for further study on the different meanings of the term 'Word of God'. See *Verbum Domini*, Catholic Truth Society, London, 2010, para. 7.

7 See RB 7:21, 33, 36–38, 41.

8 M. Magrassi, *Praying the Bible*, Liturgical Press, Collegeville, MN, 1998, p. 68.

9 Cassian, *Conferences* I, XVI–XIX.

10 Cassian, *Conferences* X, X. For a more extended teaching on Scripture in Cassian, see *Conferences* XIV.

11 D. Bonhoeffer, *Life Together*, SCM Press, London, 1954, pp. 61–4.

12 It is difficult to tell whether these books would have been books of Scripture exclusively. Benedict's 'bibliography' in RB 73 may provide some clues.

13 Some versions, for example the King James and the Vulgate, place chapter 6, 'The Letter of Jeremiah', after chapter 5 in Baruch. In the Septuagint, the 'Letter' is separated from Baruch by the book of Lamentations.

14 For more details and a contemporary expansion of this schema, see David Foster OSB, *Reading with God*, Continuum, London, 2005, p. 3.

15 Bar. 1.21; 2.5, 8, 10, 12, 24; 3.4.

16 St Hildegard of Bingen, *Liber Divinorum Operum Simplicis Hominis*, Pars I, Visio IV: *PL* 197, col. 890, C–D, and col. 891, D (my translation).

5 The blessing of worship: RB 8–20

1 Reduced to two readings in summer on account of the shorter nights. See RB 10.

2 For an accessible article on the centrality of Easter in RB, see Andrew Nugent OSB, 'Benedict's Easter', *American Benedictine Review* 54:4 (December 2003).

3 George Guiver, *Company of Voices*, SPCK, London, 1988, is a helpful guide for the non-specialist interested in the development of Christian liturgical prayer.

4 The monastic services of Lauds (at dawn), Terce (9 a.m.), Sext (noon) and None (3 p.m.) derive from this tradition.

5 For a more detailed account of the development of the liturgy in Benedict's Rule, see *RB 1980: The Rule of St Benedict*, ed. Timothy Fry OSB et al., Liturgical Press, Collegeville, MN, 1981, Appendix 3, pp. 379–414.

6 William Law, *A Serious Call to a Devout and Holy Life* (1729), Ch. XV. This definitely does *not* mean that we recite to someone who has just lost a child, for example, Job's words that the Lord gives and the Lord takes back (Job 1.21). I think Law's dictum can really only be applied by the suffering person to their own situation when, in time and the light of God's grace, they come to see a mercy in what seemed a catastrophe. We can apply it to ourselves most helpfully, with patience and sensitivity.

6 The blessing of reverence: RB 20–52

1 From George Herbert (1593–1633), 'The Elixir'.

2 Metropolitan John Zizioulas, 'Proprietors or Priests of Creation?': <www.rsesymposia.org/themedia/File/1151679350-Pergamon.pdf>.

3 D. Nicholl, *Holiness*, Darton, Longman & Todd, London, 1981, Ch. 6.

4 Nicholl, *Holiness*, p. 76.

5 Nicholl, *Holiness*, p. 106.

6 Gregory the Great, *The Dialogues*, Bk II, 36.

7 Services are longer and more elaborate on Sundays and Feast Days: Vigils comprises 12 readings, the Gospel reading, 3 canticles (i.e. chants, other than the psalms, taken from the Bible), as well as the usual 14 psalms. Benedict wishes this arrangement to stand both summer and winter. See RB 11 and 14.

7 The blessing of welcoming: RB 53–72

1 M. McGee, *Christian Martyrs for a Muslim People*, Paulist Press, Mahwah, NJ, 2008.

2 Cassian, *Institutes* Bk V, XXIV, and *Conferences* XXIV, XX.

3 The Benedictine vows are not the same as the traditional 'poverty, chastity and obedience'. Benedictines vow obedience, *conversatio morum* – difficult to translate but something like a promise to live the monastic way of life – and 'stability'.

4 S. Vanistendael, *Resilience and Spirituality: The Realism of Faith*, International Catholic Child Bureau, Geneva, 2014, p. 28.

5 See note 3 above.

8 Epilogue: The blessing of 'beyond'

1 Alfred Lord Tennyson, 'Crossing the Bar'.

2 Drawn from the *Letter to Diognetus*, paras 5 and 6.

3 'Justice' (*iustitia*) here resonates with the biblical concept of 'saving justice' (Hebrew *sedeq*) or 'righteousness'. One commentator suggests 'holiness' may be a suitable modern translation. See *RB 1980: The Rule of St Benedict*, ed. Timothy Fry OSB et al., Liturgical Press, Collegeville, MN, 1981, note to Prol. 25, p. 9.

4 A. Böckmann, *Perspectives on the Rule of St Benedict*, Liturgical Press, Collegeville, MN, 2005, pp. 77–102.

5 Jane Tyson Clement, *No One Can Stem the Tide: Selected Poems 1931–1991*, Plough Publishing House, Farmington, PA, 2000.

Copyright acknowledgements

Copyright acknowledgements

To CTBI WPCU Writers' Group for the poem, 'Re-new' on p. 28, from *Crossing Barriers*, published by Churches Together in Britain and Ireland, London, 2017, for the Week of Prayer for Christian Unity 2017.

To The Plough Publishing House for the untitled poem on p. 116, beginning 'Oh seek . . .', by Jane Tyson Clement.